89003994

BZZZ

BZZZ

A BEEKEEPER'S PRIMER

by Evelyn Fatigati

Illustrations by the author

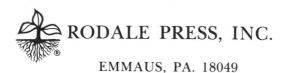

RODALE PRESS, INC.

EMMAUS, PA. 18049

2   4   6   8   10   9   7   5   3

Library of Congress Cataloging in Publication Data

Fatigati, Evelyn.
 BUZZ: a beekeeper's primer.

 SUMMARY: A young boy explains how he and his grandfather care for their bees, the hives, and honey.
 1. Bee culture—Juvenile literature. [1. Bee culture] I. Title. II. Title: A beekeeper's primer.
SF523.F33   638'.1   76-16570
ISBN 0-87857-119-1

Printed in the United States of America on recycled paper

Dedication:
For Mr. and Mrs. Nagel

Acknowledgements:
Very special thanks to Richard, who makes everything possible.

My Grandpa is a big man, and he has big hands. You might think that wouldn't be good for working with insects, but he sure does a good job as far as I can see. He's an apiarist, which is a fancy way of saying that he's a beekeeper. He's had bees forever, I think. Over 50 years at least, so you might say that he knows what he's talking about.

My name is Alan. I'm 12 years old, and I've been his helper since I was 10. He still hasn't told me everything he knows though. I guess that would take nearly as long as he's been living because he's always telling me you never stop learning about the bees. Every year is different.

I live here in my Grandpa's house with him and my grandmother, my mother and my brother, Scott. Scott is four years younger than I am, so he's not old enough to help with the bees yet. We've got a few cats living with us too. It's hard to keep track of how many there are because they're always having kittens, but Grandma says right now she feeds seven every day.

We're right on the edge of town. Our yard is great big and goes all the way down to the river. With woods on one side of us and across the road, and the river in back, it's almost like being in the country. A lot of the yard is taken up with the honey houses and the bee hives, plus we always have a big garden. And then there's Grandpa's junk collection.

A person can find just about anything he might be looking for in Grandpa's junk piles—nails, tools, buckets of hammerheads and doorknobs, pots and pans, bottles, parts of motors, old windows, screening, odds and ends of weird machinery, animal skins, all kinds of metal bits for salvaging and recycling, stacks of lumber, pieces of glass, metal crates, big bushels of foam rubber—you name it, he's got it. And I've seen almost every corner of it come in handy for someone or something at sometime. The most amazing thing of all is that Grandpa can be needing something and go directly to it. He seems to know just exactly where he's put everything.

I like it here. It seems just about perfect to me. There are lots of big trees, and I'm good at shinnying up the trunks straight to the top. It's nice in winter,

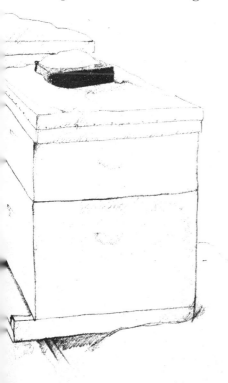

When Grandpa gave Alan his birthday present, a little "laudatory oratory" went with it. "You're wealthier than some men will ever be. You've got a hive of bees," he said.

3

but I like the spring and summer best. Of course, that's when the bees are working, and that's what I like most of all.

I've got my own hive. Grandpa gave it to me for my birthday last year. It sits near the end of the first row of hives next to the garden. I like to think that my bees like it there because it's right close to where we plant the squash, and they like squash blossoms.

When Grandpa gave me the hive, he told me it was the beginning of my wealth. "There have been times in the history of the world, Alan, when a man's fortune was measured in part by how many stands of bees he had."

Grandpa loves to talk about the bees, and when he tells me things about them he goes into what Grandma calls his "laudatory oratory." That means he's got a lot of ideas, and he's going to tell you about every one of them. He uses a lot of words to say a little bit, but he makes it lots of fun. When he gave me my hive, he went into one of his oratories.

"A man's honey stores were a symbol of security," he said, "and at times, if money was tight, he could use his honey to barter for things he needed. That golden liquid has always been considered a valuable commodity. The ancient Greeks called it the nectar of the gods, and all through written history from the Egyptians up to the present day, honey has been known to be a healthy and healing food. Of course, you and I both know that all that praise is well deserved.

"Honey is an exceptional, absolutely unique, totally

nutritious and completely satisfying treat that man enjoys with relatively little expense and almost no effort on his part. At least when we consider how much work the bees do, our end of the job seems comparatively light, wouldn't you say?

"All a man need do is supply the bees with adequate housing, and they will fly thousands of miles to do what they've done for ages and ages, even before man was on the earth. You don't even have to supply the raw materials. If the nectar-rich plants are there, the bees will fly out and find them.

"Do you know, Alan, I've read that they've put hives out on the roofs of New York City apartment buildings, and the bees have produced honey? Now you've got to know that was a lot of work, finding nectar-bearing plants in the midst of all that concrete, asphalt, bricks and mortar.

"So think of what you've got here, boy. You've got a hive of bees. What looks like a simple wooden box is a whole city of insects, a veritable sisterhood of 50,000 to 100,000 willing and highly skilled laborers who will work unceasingly from their birth to their death through two-and-a-half seasons to bring in nectar from the blooming flowers in the surrounding fields and pastures.

"Then they work inside the hive to make it into honey. They build perfect storage bins for it to ripen in, and when it's ready, all we have to do is take their surplus.

"For that kind of return, you're a rich man, Alan. Take care of your hive. It's a small fortune, but even with one stand of bees you're more wealthy than many men could ever hope to be."

I knew what Grandpa meant. I think it was the best present anybody could ever want to get, and even though I knew what the hive looked like inside I wanted to open it up right there and take a look at my very own bees. But that was impossible. My birthday is in February, and you never want to open a hive in the cold.

It's a hive just like all the others. Each one is a set of boxes without tops or bottoms, called supers, placed

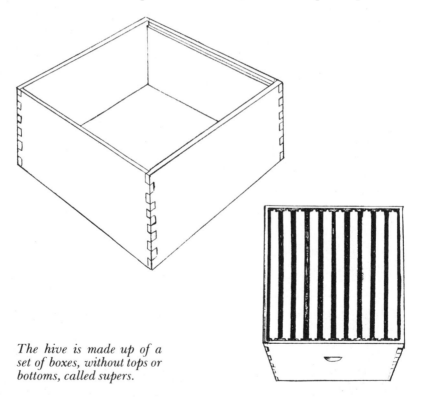

The hive is made up of a set of boxes, without tops or bottoms, called supers.

6

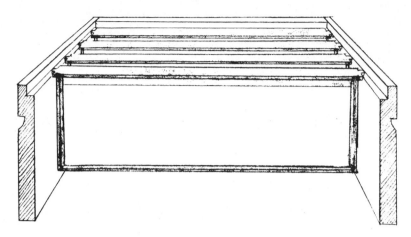

The frames hang on a grooved ledge inside the super, usually ten across.

on top of each other. Inside the supers are frames that hang on a grooved ledge. The frames can be lifted in and out, and they hold the wax foundation.

Foundation is a very thin sheet of wax that has an impression of the honeycomb pressed into it. It fits right into a frame, and it works as a base for the bees to build their honeycomb on. It helps them build straight comb, and that makes it easier for Grandpa to work with them.

Honeycomb is very fragile looking, but one pound of it can hold 25 pounds of honey. Grandpa says that the six-sided honeycomb cell is a clue to its strength, and he claims that the double comb of the honeybee—the way they build the cells back to back, out from both sides of the foundation—is one of Nature's construction marvels.

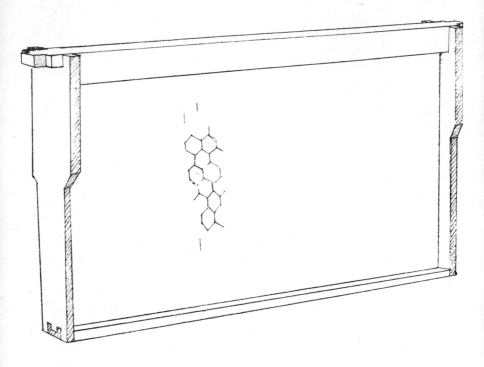

The frames hold the wax foundation that the bees use as a base for their honeycomb construction. A trough runs along the bottom of the frame (1.) to hold the foundation secure. The sides of the frame (2.) fit snugly onto the bottom so that no nails are needed. After the foundation is slipped into place, the top of the frame is nailed down.

1.

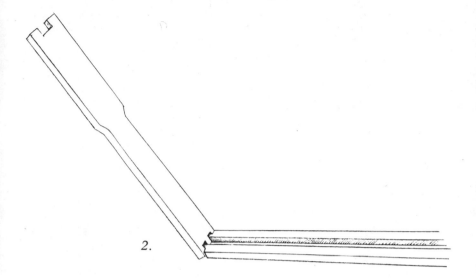

2.

Scott and I tried to count how many cells are on each side of a foundation, but we couldn't keep our eyes straight to do it. Grandpa finally helped us by counting along the bottom and one side and then multiplying. We came up with about 3,000 cells to a side of honeycomb.

That means a lot of brood nest and a lot of honey storage space in a small area. Brood nest is where they hatch their baby bees, and it's always in the bottom super called the hive body. Most supers are 10 to 12 inches deep, and they're called deep supers. The hive body is a deep super. Shallow supers are four- to six-inches deep.

All lined up beside each other, the hives look friendly. Ours are painted orange and white. I guess white is a good color for them, but last summer

In very early spring the apiary is still quiet. The honey house sits behind the hives. The mat in front of the row of hives helps to keep the weeds from growing in front of the entrances. Grandpa elevates the hives on boards or platforms to keep the bottoms dry and prevent rotting.

Grandpa got a good deal on some bright orange paint, so we've got lots of orange supers. The bees don't care, and the different colors probably help them to recognize their own hives.

The bees live in the hive body. All the ones above are for the bees to work in and store the honey. Each hive has in it one family of bees—always one queen, about 200 to 300 drones and as many as 80,000 to 100,000 worker bees.

The queen is like the mother to them all. She stays in the hive body all the time and lays eggs. She's really busy, and she can lay 2,000 eggs in a day. She gets special treatment from the workers because she's so important. They feed her, protect her, keep her clean and make sure she does her job. She's easy to spot when Grandpa opens the hive to check brood cells because she's longer and thinner than the workers.

The male bees, the drones, are big too—big and fat. "They've got to have a lot of muscle to do all that high flying," Gramps says. "Their only job the whole season long is to be ready to fertilize any young queen

(1.) The bottom board acts as the floor of the hive. (2.) The bottom super is the hive body where the brood is hatched. The queen and the drones are kept in this super by an iron grill called a queen excluder (3.) The upper supers (4. and 5.) are for storing honey. Storage supers are added as the season progresses and the bees fill them. An inner hive cover (6.) closes the hive, and the outer cover (7.), which is aluminum on top, gives protection from rain and snow.

(8.) All together the stacked supers are like stories of a building.

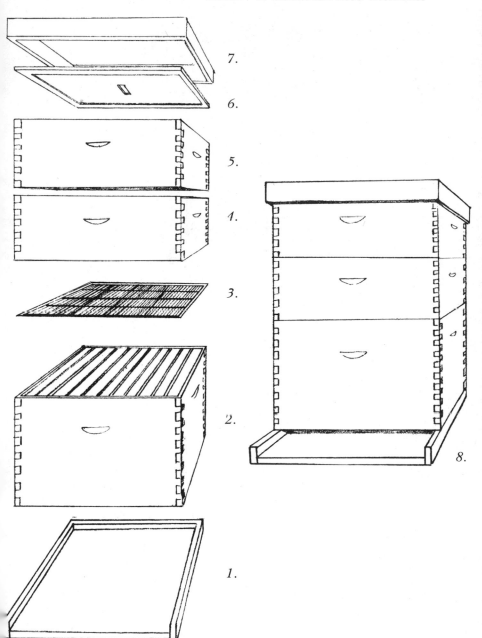

7.

6.

5.

1.

3.

2.

8.

1.

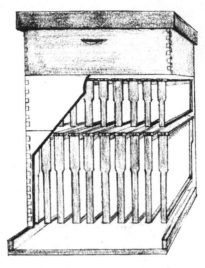

This cutaway view shows the frames hanging in the supers. Notice the spaces between each frame and between the supers allowing the bees room to work.

they may meet while they're winging around. For that they get the classic 'free ride,' if you know what I mean."

I guess I do know because all they do during the summer is eat honey, go out flying, look for queens and have a good time. For the little female workers, it's a whole different story. They just work all the time. Grandpa can go on for hours about how hard they work:

"When the worker first hatches out of the brood cell, she's as soft and downy as a baby bird and a little shaky on her legs too. The first couple of days in the

14

3.

2.

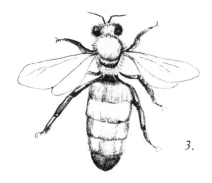

1.

The worker bee (1.) is smaller than the drone (2.) and the queen (3.).

hive she rests, just eating honey and building up her strength while her outer shell hardens. Then she's ready to begin working.

"Her first job is cleaning and polishing the brood cells, making ready for the queen to lay eggs in them again. The queen won't lay in a cell that isn't perfectly polished, so the young worker's job is important. Naturally, all of the jobs she'll be doing are important.

"Next she'll be assigned the feeding of grubs (that's what baby bees are called before they hatch). She'll feed the older grubs first because that's not as particular a job as feeding them when they're new, and she can be entrusted with it. I don't mean to say it's easy work though. Between 2,000 and 3,000 visits are involved to raise one baby bee larva. Multiply that times the number of bees in the hive, and you might get an idea about how busy these young workers are. It's a figure that would boggle the ordinary brain of the everyday man in the street."

Grandpa always is trying to "boggle my brain" with some amazing fact about the bees. He's been pretty good at it so far. I don't know where he digs up all that information.

"After about a week she can feed the young larvae. It's about this time that she'll take her first flight, try out her wings and figure out what they're all about. You've seen these novices, Alan. In the afternoon when the sun is warm, they're right there in front of the hive, hovering over the entrance, getting their bearings and seeing what the world is like. It comes

The bee larvae are cradled in individual cells, each one with a ration of royal jelly that it feeds on during its gestation period. The very small larvae pictured are just a day or two old. For six days nurse bees feed them. After six days they seal the cells. Those with domed caps like the ones in the lower right hand corner are the larger drone larvae. The flat caps are cells containing worker larvae.

From the time the cells are sealed by the worker bees, it takes approximately two weeks for the brood to hatch–slightly longer for the drones. At the upper left a baby bee emerges from its cell.

17

naturally to them, and pretty soon they're back inside working at odd jobs. They take the loads from the field workers as they arrive and deposit them in storage cells, pack pollen into the pollen cells, clean litter and dead bees from the hive and work in teams to ventilate the hive and brew honey.

"But all these jobs are just a sort of break before a worker takes her post building comb. As a builder she'll eat lots of honey. It takes honey to make wax, and the bees eat seven pounds of it for every pound of honeycomb they're able to build."

Grandpa has shown me the wax plates on the underside of the bee. The beeswax oozes out of these wax plates, then hardens into little chips, and the bees rub it off of their abdomens with their legs. Then they pass it up to their mouths and sort of chew it up to soften it, so they can mold it into place with their tongues.

"See how they build the comb so that it slants slightly upward?" Grandpa said. "That keeps the honey from running out. They think of everything, don't they, boy?

"After she's made wax—and the bees do that only when the weather is warm and if more comb is needed—that little apprentice worker may find herself on guard duty."

I've seen these guards at the entrance to the hive checking out the smell of every worker coming through. Usually they're pretty sharp and hard to fool. It's fun to see them in action, like real soldiers.

18

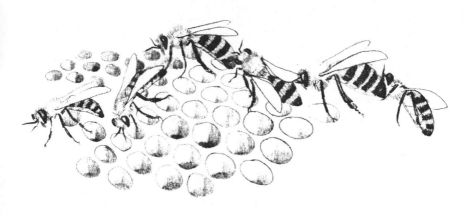

Workers engaged in making wax cling to each other in long chains, sometimes for as long as 24 hours. When the heat from their closely strung bodies and the honey they have eaten combine in a chemical reaction, eight tiny pockets on their abdomens begin to ooze wax. Each worker pokes the wax out of the pockets with her legs and passes it forward to her mouth. She chews it and mixes it with her saliva until it is a proper consistency for modeling. Then she plasters the bit of wax onto the foundation. As each bee contributes again and again, the honeycomb takes shape.

No worker from another hive can get past them. The guards recognize their own hive odor and send foreigners on their way. If a strange bee gets into the hive, it's a bad thing because she could start robbing. But that's a long story, and I'll tell you about it later.

"She may take over as fanner too," Grandpa told me. "Standing at the entrance with her wings moving so fast you can't see them, she fans air into the hive to evaporate moisture out of the nectar.

"Finally that little worker is ready to go out into the fields. It must be a pretty heady feeling for her, Alan. Just think, it's the first time she flies away from the hive and lands on one of those heavenly clover blossoms, rich with sweet juices and dusty with pollen. She's out under the blue summer sky, the sun is warm, and she's among friends.

"In the field the bees are polite. Not too many to one flower. They wait their turn if the flowers are crowded or move on to find an empty one. Even though they're from different hives, they behave like sisters when they're in the field. Only at home, when they have to protect their stores, are they feisty.

"On her foraging trips she loads up with pollen on her legs or nectar in her nectar sacs and heads back to her hive. She's been gone maybe an hour visiting 50 or more flowers. She deposits her load with a house bee, who is one of her younger sisters, and takes a rest before she goes out again.

"Some field bees are water foragers since water is a crucial ingredient to the hive's well-being and because

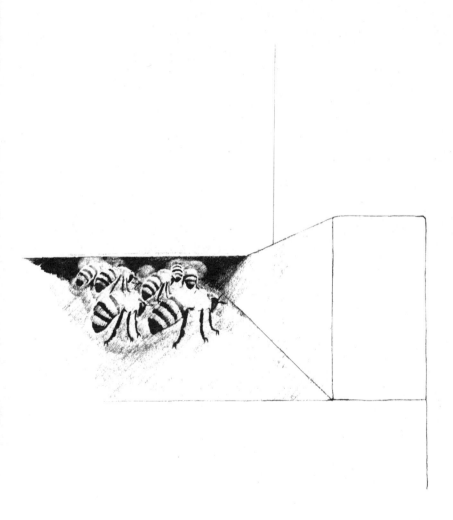

Fanners are posted at the hive posters.

they use it to make their bee food. It's a busy life inside and outside the hive, that's for sure. She's a mighty fine creature who works so hard and gives us so much." Grandpa made me understand that.

Bees tie a man down, Grandpa says, but I don't see how there could be nicer work. You get to be outside when it's nice, and in the wintertime they don't take much tending, just a check now and then to be sure they've got enough feed. Grandpa lifts them a little to see how heavy they are. That's how he tells if they're O.K.

During the winter, my hive had just one shallow super on it because that was enough to see them through—about 35 pounds of honey. I guess bees never sleep. Even during the winter they get together in the center of the hive in a kind of ball we call a cluster and move around just a very little bit. That's how they keep each other warm.

If the weather warms up enough, like on those slushy days, they'll come out of the hive for a little cleansing flight. Bees won't dirty the inside of their hive, so they wait for a nice day to fly out. Then the snow all around the hive has little brown dots on it from bee droppings. In the early spring, Grandma has to be careful about hanging out the wash on the clothesline because they'll stain the clothes with it.

"It's just honey and pollen. That's all it is, is bee bread," Gramps says, "but it sure does stain. Can't get it out for anything. And they really go for that white."

On those nice days when it's 30 to 40 degrees, I worry about the bees. If they fly out too far, they might not make it back home. If they land in the snow, sometimes their feet get cold, and they can't pick themselves up again. Whenever we see one stranded in the snow, we pick her up. She'll warm herself in our hands and fly away like new.

If we ever do have to feed them before the winter is over, we use a bottle feeder that fits right into the hive. That way they don't have to come outside. But it's best not to have to feed them during the cold months. We try to leave them enough honey in the fall to last until it warms up in the spring. Just in case though, Grandpa always has some old honey around to use as feed.

"Some fellows will feed their bees sugar and water, or corn syrup and water, but I'll tell you, Alan, I think it's a crime. Such sugars aren't fit for bees to eat, or humans either for that matter. And there's no creature more deserving of honey than the honeybee herself. She works hard enough for it; she ought to be able to enjoy it. Sugar makes inferior honey and can cause some digestive troubles for the bees."

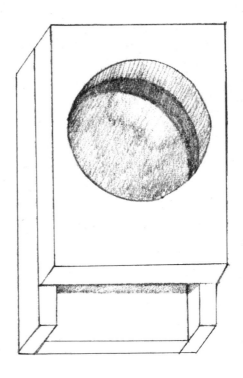

The bottle feeder is a small wooden box with a round hole in the top for the neck of the bottle.

One side is open and slides in under the doorway of the hive. The bees can enter the box from the inside and drink from the perforations in the jar lid.

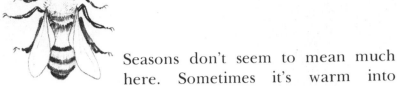Seasons don't seem to mean much here. Sometimes it's warm into November, doesn't snow till the middle of January, and some years we've had the worst blizzard of the year in April. When we get snowed in, I like to look through the bee equipment catalogues. They're chock full of all kinds of weird gadgets and tools for working with the hives. Looking at all the stuff is interesting, but I think Grandpa makes it a lot more simple. All he uses is a bee veil and a hive tool.

The bee veil is a netting that fits over his hat to protect his face. The hive tool is a steel bar with a curved lip at one end. It fits into your hand like a knife, and it comes in handy all the time. There are a dozen or more uses for it. It's a regular "all-purpose" tool.

Grandpa's had everything he needs for so long that he hardly ever orders anything new except jars, foundation, and sometimes frames. Last year he decided to get a new smoker though. Smoke helps to calm the bees if they get peevish when we're looking in on them. They think their hive is on fire, and they start eating honey so they have some food to go on if they have to fly away. At least that's how Grandpa says the smoke works. It's kind of like food for the road, he says, and bees full of honey aren't so likely to be stinging, mad bees.

Every few years Grandpa has to get a bee veil too.

When he does, I get his old one. That's one piece of equipment Grandpa does wear and makes me wear. It's important to protect your eyes and face.

By the looks of some guys when they work, you'd think they were going to battle, all armored up from head to toes in big, clumsy suits. That's not needed if

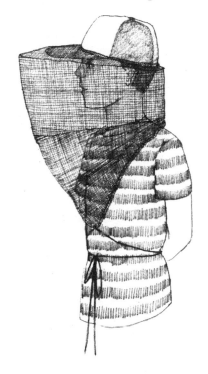

Every beekeeper needs a bee veil. Wire mesh screening makes a rigid frame, and netting encloses the face and neck. This bee veil is designed to wear with a hat. Grandpa always wears a hat when he works with the bees. The cap secures his hair, so if a bee lands on his head she can fly away without getting her wings tangled in his hair.

The hive tool is an all-purpose tool. The flat end works as a knife, a scraper, a wedge. The curved end can be used like a small crowbar. The hole with the slits in the center is used to pry up nails.

you handle the frames and supers gently, don't jerk or move too fast and always are careful not to set any edges or lids down on any of the bees.

I've never seen Grandpa wear anything but a veil. When he's just checking the bees and it's a nice day, he doesn't even wear that always. He never wears gloves. It's really something to see. When I'm bigger—you have to be strong to lift those heavy supers smoothly—I want to handle them as well as he does.

When I sent the order out for one smoker, one veil, 20 cases of five-pound jars for extracted honey and 10 cases of two-and-a-half pound jars for comb honey, I put two conservation stamps on the back of

The smoker is an essential aid to the beekeeper. Grandpa burns a coil of cardboard inside the tin. By squeezing the bellows (2.), air is forced into the smoker and up through the grating on which the cardboard is burning. Air continues up the tin and blows smoke out of the spout. The arrow (3.) points to the small hole in the bellows that lets air current into the smoker.

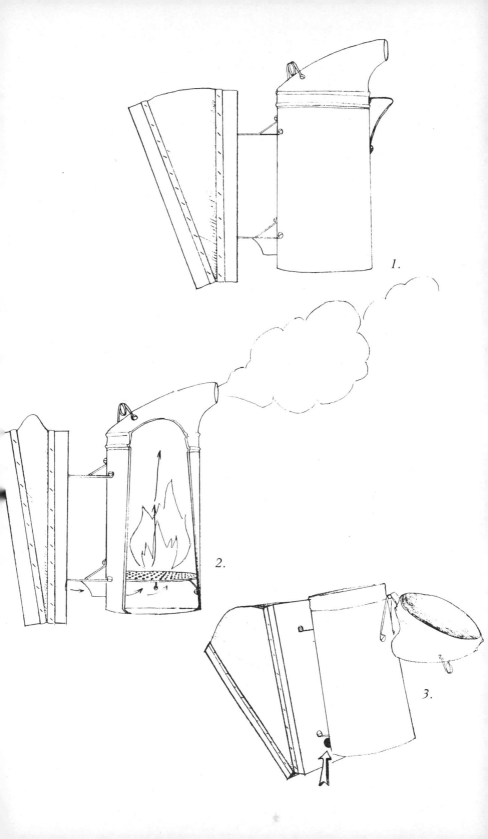

1.

2.

3.

the envelope, one with a monarch butterfly and one with a mountain lion. For postage I used a 10-cent Kansas wheat stamp that shows a wheat field with a train going through it. I collect stamps, and I like to use stickers and picture stamps on my letters.

Around the middle of April we can finally count on some nice weather, and the bees can start to get out and into the neighborhood. The mornings warm up enough for us to be out working too, and one of the first jobs of the season is cleaning frames.

All the old frames that have been used for brood nests for a few years and aren't in really good shape, or any frames with foundation that have been damaged, Grandpa hauls out of storage to clean. He cuts the comb and foundation out of the frame and scrapes the wax and propolis off the edges with a wire scrubber. Propolis is a sticky wax the bees make and use for glue. I wash it in sudsy water, rinse it off and hang it up to dry.

It's a pretty messy job, so we wear our oldest blue jeans and do it out under the trees in a kind of lean-to Grandpa built. The bees can smell the honeycomb, and they fly all around our heads looking for honey and snooping around in the comb.

We collect quite a pile of wax, and Grandpa saves every smidgen bit of it so he can send it off to be recy-

As a part of spring cleaning, young workers carry out dead bees who didn't live through the winter.

31

cled. The bee equipment company in Illinois melts it down and makes new foundation with it. Beeswax is expensive, so Grandpa can save a lot of money by sending his old wax away. That way he gets a discount on the foundation that he buys. There's nobody better at saving money by reusing old stuff or by remaking it into new than Grandpa.

We clean supers just like we do frames. Grandpa scrapes the wax off and scours them. I wash and rinse them and hang them up to dry. It's another spring job that we do, so we can be ready to stack them up on the hives when the weather gets nice.

While he's scraping off the propolis with his hive tool, Grandpa checks the supers for moth eggs. Hopefully, he won't find any because it's not a good sign if he does. The moth gets into the supers and lays eggs there. She flies away, but the moth larvae hatch out and eat the honeycomb. They tunnel right through it and leave a silky strand that really makes a mess of the comb.

We've usually been lucky. If the bee colony is strong enough and those guards are on their duty, the moths won't be able to get into the hive. Some beekeepers spray their hives with a moth poison to keep them out, but Grandpa would never do that.

"It ruins the taste of the honey, it's not good for the bees and it's not good for the environment," he says. "This use of chemicals and pesticides is a dangerous business. It's killing the birds that eat the bugs, and the pests and diseases just get hardier. It's upset the balance of nature. Forty years ago we didn't have this much trouble with crop diseases and insect pests.

"It's murder for the bees—weakens them terribly. It's killing them off, and we've got to have the bee if we want to eat. The bee pollinates the blossoms that make the fruit. Some folks would say that bees' honey is only a minor part of their value to us. Why, if it weren't for the honeybee, we wouldn't have apples, peaches, pears, apricots, not to mention melons, plums, cherries, berries, all manner of blossoming fruits and vegetables, plus hundreds of varieties of gorgeous flowers.

"It's truly a crime the way we treat her in return. If the honeybee can't thrive, then neither can we. If man does succeed in poisoning her into extinction, he'll miss her when she's gone. Mark my words!"

Grandpa doesn't use any kind of chemicals. We never put any on the garden. And if we have any bug troubles, Grandpa makes a garlic spray for a remedy.

In April or May Gramps checks each hive to make sure it has a queen excluder in it. That's a wire grill that keeps the queen and the drones out of the upper supers. The wires are far enough apart that workers can get through it, but the fat drones and the big queen can't. It fits right on top of the hive body under the upper supers.

We don't want the queen to get into the supers because she'll lay eggs in them, and that's not good for extracting. She's best confined to the hive body. We don't like the drones in there either because they aren't careful about making their bee droppings outside of the hive, and that stains the honeycomb.

One other spring job depends on when the foundation gets here from Illinois. When it comes, for about a week every night after school I put new foundation into the cleaned up frames. I like to put in foundation. The frames always look so clean and new with the creamy-colored foundation in them.

I use a little hammer to tack the frame back into place, and Scott helps me. We've got a system, and we're pretty fast. He hands me the foundation, I put it in, hammer the frame together and he stacks the finished frames up. It's a good job for us.

Things start picking up for us beekeepers in May. From then until sometimes as late as July, there's the possibility that the bees might swarm. It's their way of increasing and multiplying. But it's not good for honey production, and as Grandpa says, that's the business we're in.

When the bees swarm, the bee colony splits in two. Then one half stays in the old home, and one half has to find a new one. The half that leaves builds comb and brood and spends its time getting set up again. All this is happening when the flowers are beginning to produce nectar and a full strength hive would be making honey.

Grandpa knows all the signs, and we try to prevent it. We watch for swarming pretty closely. It's important to make sure the bees aren't crowded and to give them supers for honey storage. That way we get them to thinking about making honey instead of swarming.

In the early spring the queen starts laying eggs, and the workers fetch pollen and water to make the jelly they feed to the larvae. It takes 21 days for larvae to hatch into worker bees, and as they hatch, the queen lays more eggs. The colony can get pretty large in a short time with a good queen.

Of course, that's the idea. The hive needs to have lots of workers ready, when the first honey flow comes on. Actually, the honey flow could be called a

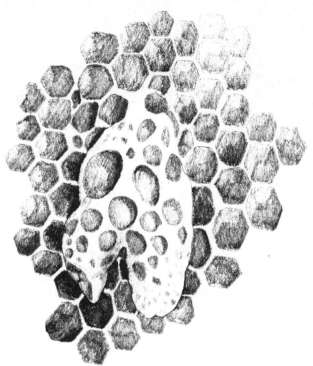

The queen cell resembles a peanut shell protruding from the brood comb. These two are joined together. The left side has not been completed yet.

nectar flow. It comes when one type of flower is producing a lot of nectar. At certain times during the season, different plants make more nectar than usual. The bees stay with those plants until the flow is over. Honey flows are important because that's what makes the honey surplus, so that we can have some. The first honey flow around here is the dandelion flow.

We always like the honey flow to come early because if there's nectar to be gathered, the bees won't think about swarming. But if the weather makes the flow come late or if the flow is a short one, the bees might start building queen cells. That usually means that they're getting ready to swarm.

Queen cells are easy to spot, and Grandpa and I check through a few of the hive bodies to look for them. He says he doesn't know how it's decided in the hive that a group of workers should start making these weird-looking cells. It's just part of nature. Queen cells are big, and they look kind of like a peanut shell hanging down from the brood frames. The bees usually make a few at a time so that the bees who stay behind—mostly the newly hatched ones— are sure to have a queen.

They get the queen to lay an egg in each one of these queen cells even though she may not want to do it, and they feed the larvae royal jelly. Worker bee larvae are fed only enough bee bread to make them workers. But the queen larvae get lots and lots of it, more than they can eat maybe. That's what makes them queens.

Grandpa says royal jelly is pretty neat stuff. "It's produced in the heads of the worker bees, who then feed it to the larvae. After six days on this diet, the grubs are 1,500 times their original size. Sounds like magic food, doesn't it, Alan? People have thought so for centuries, and they've always tried to get it from the bees. There are even places you can buy it nowadays, but it's mighty expensive. Folks think it will make them young again, and ladies put it on their faces and eyelids because they think it will keep their skin from wrinkling. I've heard people prescribe it for every curious ailment and swear it was the only think that could cure their ills."

A swarm of bees most often will cluster onto a low hanging branch of a tree. Sometimes the swarm is so heavy that the branch breaks.

I've never tasted the stuff, but Grandpa jokes with Mom and Grandma about it, tells them he can make them beautiful and young and all that. I don't know though. I like them just fine the way they are.

If our timing is just right, Grandpa and I can open the hives, check for these queen cells and pick out the ones we find. That's one way of preventing swarming. We don't have to do this for every hive every year. The bees swarm only if their queen is old (that's three, four, sometimes five years old for bees), if she dies or is diseased, or if they're too cramped.

When they're swarming because their queen is old, Grandpa gives them a new queen and saves them the swarming energy. That's a whole operation that's fun to watch. He has to put her in a little cage in the hive, while the bees get used to her and her new smell. She's sealed into her cage by a block of sugar, and the bees eat through the sugar to get at her. By the time they've done that, they've usually decided they like her well enough. Then she comes out and starts working right away.

If we don't catch the new queens before they hatch, the old queen and about half of the hive—mostly the older bees who lived through the winter—load themselves with honey. In the early afternoon on a sunny day they'll rush out of the hive and fly into the sky in big circles, until they see something to land on.

They can land just about anywhere. Grandpa loves to tell stories about some of the odd places he's picked them up. He's the beeman in town, and whenever anybody has a swarm of bees land in their yard they call him. He's picked them off of store fronts, water hydrants, backyard fences, front porch pillars, swing sets, clotheslines and once from a scarecrow. He says he's even picked them off the arm of a man, but I've never known whether to believe that story or not. Mostly they just land on a tree limb or maybe a fence

"Swarming must be a happy time for the bees because they're so congenial," Grandpa says. "When they land, they form a cluster. All clinging to each other there in a big ball, they seem just as tickled as punch. They won't sting when they're in the swarming cluster, but when people call me they're all flustered and panicked. They've herded their children inside and they act like they've got a monster loose in their back yard.

"But bees in the cluster are just like a cuddly baby. They're full of honey, they're excited about finding a new home and wouldn't hurt a flea. The good Lord was looking after us beekeepers a long time ago, I guess, because it sure makes the job easier for us."

What Grandpa does to hive a swarm is take along a hive body with him that's got a few frames of capped honey in it. He sets that down and then finds the queen in the cluster. He puts her into the hive, and pretty soon the swarm follows her right in. When they're all inside Grandpa can put them in the back of his truck and bring them home. Just as easy as that he's added another colony to his apiary. Grandpa says that with fifty-some hives now we don't need any-

This swarm of bees was so heavy that the branch broke under the weight of them. After Grandpa cuts the limb off at the break, he'll shake the bees onto the canvas spread out for them. The white background helps him to spot the queen more easily. When he finds her, he puts her into the hive. Then the swarm will follow her inside.

more, but people keep calling him. He can't stand to see a swarm destroyed.

Mostly we try to keep our bees here from swarming. In fact, Grandpa is so good at guessing their swarming instinct that I've only seen them do it once or twice. He just keeps his eyes on them, watching for any clustering on the outside of the hive. He knows what to watch for in the weather, keeps supers on the hives as they need them and hopes for an early dandelion flow.

We're always glad to see those "weeds" come up. Grandma doesn't even let me mow until after they go to seed. I really can't see why people are so crazy about getting rid of dandelions anyway. They're not so bad to look at, and they don't last long enough to be a real weed. Grandma says she can remember her mother fixing dandelion greens for supper and drying the root for a medicine, so they must be good for something.

I gave a talk in my class at school telling a little about the bees, and I asked everybody to ask their parents not to spray the dandelions, poison the roots or dig them up. The poison kills the bees when they drink it up with the nectar. Maybe if people thought more from a bee's point of view they wouldn't use the poisons.

Grandpa usually puts at least one hive on a scale in order to see how much nectar the bees bring in at various times during the season.

Most years Grandpa puts a hive on a scale, so he can keep a daily record of how much honey the bees bring in. He's got a big industrial scale down by the river, and that's where he puts the hive. He records the weight both at night and in the morning, to tell how much water the bees fanned out of the nectar.

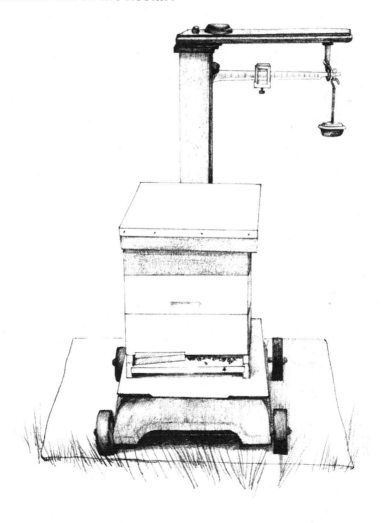

The dandelion honey flow begins as soon as the yellow flowers reach full bloom. That's when the nectar begins to flow, and it's usually around the first to the middle of May. The mornings are still crisp, but early scouts get out and fly around in the neighborhood looking for dandelion fields.

When they come back to the hive, they do a dance on the honeycomb. The dance tells the worker bees in what direction the flow is, how far from the hive it is and how much is there. Grandpa and I have seen them do the dance. Some workers pick up on the dance and repeat it to others. By this time the sun is up and the mornings are pretty warm; it's a good time for the bees to work.

Their best hours for working are between 10 in the morning and 2 in the afternoon when the sun is warmest. An ideal day is when the thermometer says 85 degrees and there's a slight breeze. During honey flows though, they'll work thick and fast from sunup to sundown to get all they can while the flow lasts.

That's when you can see their flying route, as if it were drawn in the sky. It's called a fly line. Up close at the door of the hive it looks like a jet port with landings and takeoffs every second. Grandpa says every time they land there, it's one drop of honey. Sometimes there are so many of them at the entrance that there's a mass of bees hovering in the air in front waiting to get in. But they never mistake each other's hives. They know which one is their own and fly right to it.

Some of the bees bring in pollen instead of nectar. You can see the yellow clumps on their back legs. It's really packed on, and I don't see how they can carry all that weight or walk with the bulge.

Workers collect pollen on their hind legs.

Grandpa says the bees can't carry nectar and pollen at the same time, but this bee, her legs loaded with pollen, seems to be drinking nectar from a clover blossom.

Pollen and nectar aren't the same thing. Grandpa told me a long time ago the difference between the two. Pollen is the yellow dust from the blossom and flowering part of a plant. "It's this dust that fertilizes the flowers that make the fruits we eat," he said. "Apples, grapefruit, oranges, tangerines, squashes, pumpkins, peas, corn, alfalfa, and buckwheat, plus hundreds more."

48

I told him that all of those things weren't fruits, but he said, "Fruit of the vine, boy. Fruit of the vine. It's a way of speaking."

The bees can't make honey from pollen. They use it for food. Their legs are really hairy, so that the pollen sticks to them. They pack it on, and as they fly from plant to plant, some of it falls off and onto the flowers. That way they fertilize plants that can't fertilize themselves.

"That's why bees are so important to the farmer," Grandpa says. "That's why they're so important to all of us. If it weren't for the work of the bees, Alan, the world would be a poorer place indeed. Poorer by at least a thousand known fruits and vegetables. That's why I'm against the use of pesticides and all this chemical farming: because it's killing the bees, and if the bees don't eat, we don't eat."

Nectar is the sweet, sticky juice in the flower of the plant. Grandpa says that hundreds of thousands of years ago, plants developed nectar to attract the bees to their flowers. The bees would pick up the pollen while they were drinking the nectar. This was a favor to the plant since it couldn't get up and walk over to the other plants by itself. The arrangement worked out, and they've been at it ever since.

The bees drink up the nectar. They have special nectar sacs inside their bodies where they carry the juice. "Some folks will say the bees can gather both at once, Alan, but I've yet to understand how they can carry all that. They don't have trailers, you know."

49

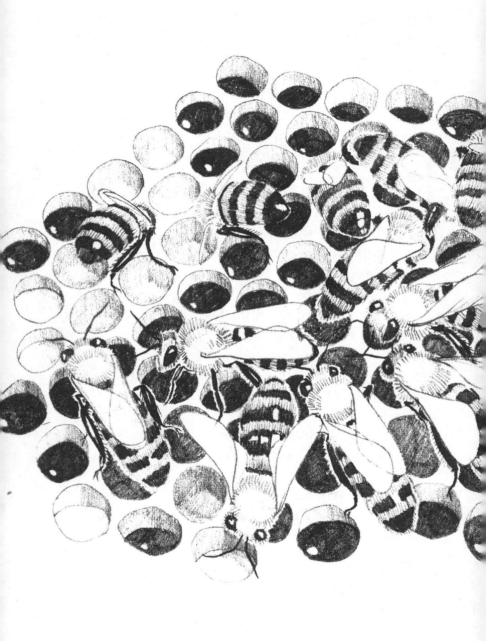

Young house bees take the nectar from the field workers and store it in the upper supers. Pollen is also stored in the comb along side the honey. The two cells at upper right contain pollen.

At night workers fan air through the hive to evaporate moisture out of the nectar. Inside the hive and at the entrance, they stand and move their wings so fast they seem not to have any at all. Other workers stand in the currents of air created by the fanners and dip their tongues into the honey stores. Each holds a drop of honey on the tip of her tongue, while the air circulates and evaporates the water out of it. This process is repeated, and, drop by drop, the nectar is condensed into honey.

When Grandpa said that, I got a pretty funny picture in my head of bees with little red wagons tied onto them flying out of the hive.

Bees gather a lot more nectar than they do pollen. Nectar is what they make into honey. When the field worker comes back to the hive loaded with nectar, she gives it to one of the younger house bees to take care of. Making honey is a complicated process, but Grandpa is good at explaining it.

"This house bee takes her load of nectar to a place where she'll be right in the current of air that workers are fanning into the hive—fanning is what evaporates the water out of the nectar, Alan.

"Drop by drop she'll put a little on her tongue from her own nectar sac. She swallows the nectar and brings up another drop. She does this about 80 or 90 times every 20 minutes.

"When she's satisfied that it's the right consistency, she puts the load into a storage cell. And at night she'll go back and do it all over again. When enough water has been evaporated out of the nectar and it's just the right consistency, the workers will cap the honey cell and let it ripen.

"That, my boy, is what honey is: The pure sweet nectar of millions of blossoms condensed to a right and proper consistency known only to those bees who tend it. The time allowed for ripening is important, but once sealed inside the miraculous honeycomb and kept away from moisture, it will keep indefinitely.

"Do you know that when they opened the Great Pyramid of Cheops in the Egyptian desert they found jugs of honey buried there with the Pharoah thousands of years ago, and the honey was still edible? Think of it: The nectar of ancient flowers preserved for centuries and centuries!

"No germs can grow in honey, and if stored properly it will not spoil, will not rot, will not ferment. I'll tell you, it almost makes a man believe it is a magical substance."

The dandelion flow was a good one. According to the scale, the bees brought in five and six pounds of honey every day for a week and a half. The bees in my hive filled one shallow super. If the other hives did as well, they'd all be in pretty good shape. All they needed after that was a warm and sunny June. We missed the mark there though. It was cold and damp.

Farmers had a bad time through June too. Some had to plant a second time because the first planting rotted in the fields. If the seeds get too wet when they're just shoots in the ground, they'll drown like anything else. Grandpa's brother, Hilmer, is a farmer, Grandpa used to farm, and my mother grew up on the farm; so we're all interested in how the farmers do.

The dampness was bad for the clover flow that comes after the dandelions. Grandpa relies on the white clover because the honey from it is just about the clearest and sweetest you'd ever want to taste. There's a lot of it around here. The cows graze on it. It even grows on people's lawns.

But we didn't have any luck with the clover. There was no nectar in it. We had a couple of early morning fogs, and Grandpa thinks that the fog carries with it all the sprays and pesticides that everybody uses in the early summer. The fog is like a low cloud. When it settles on the clover, it leaves all that junk on it and ruins the nectar.

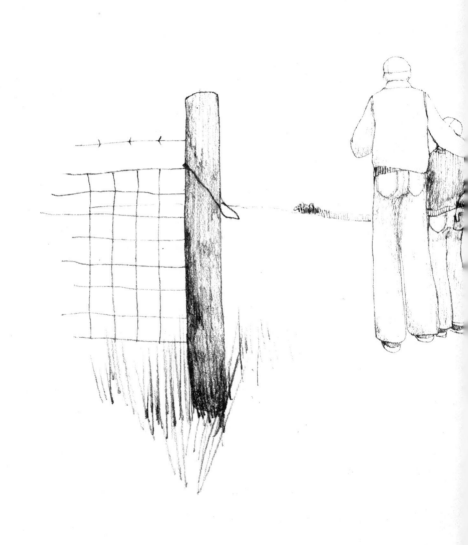

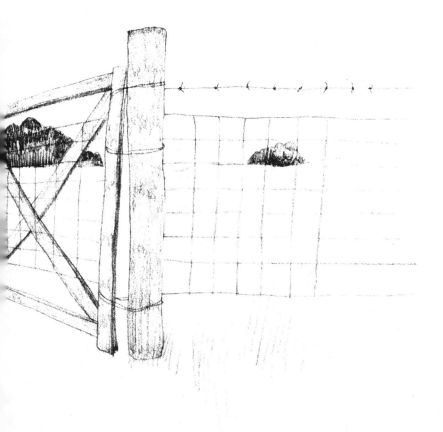

Grandpa and Alan would drive into the country and walk through the fields looking for bees working the clover.

We'd go driving out into the country and walk through some of the fields to see if there were any bees in it. We saw plenty of clover but not one bee.

"If there was nectar in it, you could bet we'd see those girls out here," Grandpa would say.

After that miserable month—six out of ten of my
Little League baseball games were rained out, so
you've got to know it was a bad month—July started
out really hot. There still wasn't much nectar gathering for the bees, and a few of the hives turned to
swarming, mine included.

One day before lunch I found them hanging outside of the hive. I told Gramps about it at the lunch table, but he said they were just cooling off in this hot
weather. I kept my eye on them anyway, and after the
sun went down there were still bees hanging there in
a clump right outside the entrance. I showed them to
Grandpa, and he said in that case it was time to check
on them.

The next day was hot and windy. As soon as we
lifted that inner cover, bees oozed out like a pot
overflowing. They just boiled up out of the hive, and
I couldn't figure out how Grandpa was going to get a
super back on without crushing hundreds of bees.

Grandpa stayed cool—he always does. "Give them a
little smoke, Alan. I guess I should've known they'd
all be home on a day like today," he said. You've got
to be a calm person to be a good beekeeper.

We took the winter super off and found it nearly
full again with the dandelion honey. There were still
so many bees inside that we had to use the smoker

*The bees were hanging out of Alan's hive, indicating it was time to check
the brood comb for queen cells.*

59

Working slowly, without fast, jerking movements, Grandpa can check through the hive without wearing a bee veil.

twice, and the hive body was jammed full of them. Grandpa took off the queen excluder, after he scraped away all the bridge work the bees had made.

The bees build up the honeycomb to connect the frames between the supers and that's called bridge

This cross section of a hive illustrates how the bees connect the frames of one super to the frames in the supers above and below. The bridge work acts much like a stairway, and the bees use it to travel up and down through the honeycomb.

work. There's honey in it, so as soon as you scrape it away the honey drips out and the bees get right in there to clean it up.

"These girls are the fussiest housekeepers," Grandpa said. "They can't even wait till we're through here to clean up, and they can lick a plate clean better and faster than any slickersnout you ever saw." He calls me and Scott slickersnouts because we like sweets so much and because of the way we go after the cappings in the honey house. That's when we're extracting, a long time away from July.

It was a touchy job with all those workers at home. A few times they stung Grandpa's hands. "Doesn't hurt at all, Alan," he claimed, "and it helps my rheumatism. It's my own fault anyway. I just got in their way, wouldn't you say?"

The bees were so crowded in the supers that they'd even put honey in the cells on the brood frames. Grandpa loosened the frames and then very slowly picked them up one at a time out of the hive body. While he held them up, we looked over both sides for any queen cells. The queen is slightly bigger and thinner than the other bees, and if I look really good I can usually spot her. Grandpa's better at it than I am, but he doesn't give her away. Sometimes we'll get through the brood frames though, and just to check me out he'll say, "Did you see her up in the left hand corner of the fifth frame?"

I found her this time on the fourth frame that he pulled out. We found the beginnings of four queen cells too, just as we'd suspected. They're much bigger than the other cells and are easy to see. Gramps just picked them off with his fingers. Only one had a larva in it.

"You've got a good queen working in there for you, Alan." He said he could tell because the brood cells were nearly all full of larvae. "She's a tidy layer too. See how she's worked in a spiral out from the center, with all the cells in between filled in? A good queen always lays her eggs systematically like that."

He estimated that I'd have about 30,000 new bees hatching in the next fourteen days and told me that that was pretty hot returns on my "investment." He's always saying, "You're a wealthy man, Alan. And what a unique and singularly resourceful wealth it is. You've got a hive of bees!"

The hot weather, their crowded conditions plus the fact that there wasn't much nectar in the fields caused the bees to get the swarming urge. But Grandpa said there were a couple of things we could do to stop it. For one, we could put a queen excluder trap over the door of the hive. Then when the new queen hatches, the old one can't get out and the two girls have to fight it out. They would fight to the finish. Grandpa says it's their nature—that's the way they operate.

The queen trap only goes on if we don't want to go through the brood nest, but since we'd already done that, that method was out.

The best thing to do was just give them more supers. As long as they have room, they'll keep working to fill those supers. I liked this idea better than the trap because it meant more honey. Grandpa agreed with me there, and we put on two shallow supers full of frames and new foundation. They went right on top of the hive body. The full one that we had already taken off we put on top of the two new ones. You always put the empty supers closest to the brood cell. That way the bees don't have to travel up through full supers to get to the empty ones they're working in.

Grandpa says you've always got to be thinking of the bees like this and trying to save them time. That's why he's really careful about keeping the frames and supers clean and the foundation and honeycomb in good shape. It saves the bees work, and saving them work saves them time to make more honey.

We had to wait until night when all the bees had gone inside to close up my hive. They could all fit in then. Grandpa said they'd be O.K. after that, but we kept a watch on them for the next week or so just to make sure we'd caught their swarming urge in time.

Bees are real fiends for keeping things clean. Every morning they clean out their hive. They drag out any dead bees or bits of dirt, and they even sweep their doorstep clean with their tongues. Grandpa says they're the cleanest creatures on earth.

"They appreciate the favor in return, too," he says. "They don't like people working with them who are dirty or smelly with sweat and grime. They don't like the odor of cigarettes, can't stand the smell of beer or alcohol, and they're none too partial to the smell of cats and dogs. They get pesky."

Grandpa always reminds me of this whenever I come out to help him. He makes me go inside to wash my hands with soap, especially when I've been playing with the cats. I can't see why he has to worry about it too much though. He smells just like honeycomb no matter how much he washes. Even after Grandma washes his clothes, he smells like bees and honey. I wish I knew how he does it because I'd like to smell that good too. He says it comes with the years. "It gets into a man's pores," he says.

Bees are so crazy about working and keeping clean that when there isn't much nectar to gather or flying conditions aren't right, they'll start "scrubbing." At least that's what Grandpa calls it. They just clean all over the hive inside and out, over and over again, even when there's nothing to clean anymore.

If there is no nectar to be gathered in the fields, sometimes a hive will start scrubbing. With their tongues the workers clean the front of the hive and entryway, removing every speck of dust. Just to keep themselves busy, they will clean it and reclean it long after the dirt has been swept away.

The mat in front of the platform keeps the weeds down, so the bees have a clear flying line into the hive.

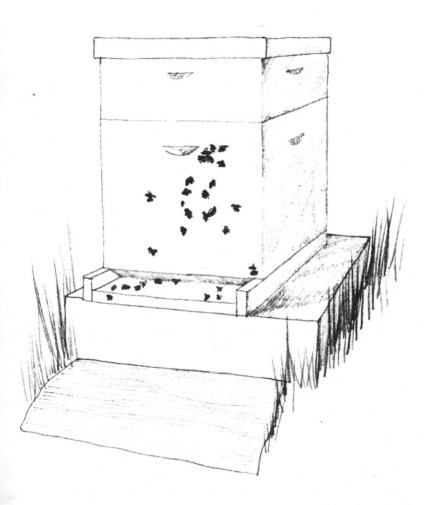

July was hot and dry, and the heat dried up the nectar flow. One hive especially was scrubbing like a troop of janitors for a couple of days. They were all over the outside, crawling over the front, picking up every little speck of anything they could find. When they finished it once, they'd do it again.

Grandpa was getting pretty disgusted with them. He thought they should be out looking for nectar. On the third day at supper, he finally said, "If they're at it again tomorrow, I'm going to fool those fool bees."

The next day they were still at it, so he got out a roll of cellophane. "I'll wrap this around the hive, and it'll make it so slippery they won't be able to climb up there and waste time at this scrubbing business."

The joke was on Grandpa. The bees just came out of their door and climbed right up the cellophane and started scrubbing it!

"It just goes to show you what worthless behavior that scrubbing really is," Grandpa said. He was satisfied because at least it had proven that. We knew there couldn't be anything on that cellophane worth picking over, but there they were, crawling over it, sweeping it clean with their tongues. Maybe they could see something we couldn't. We all decided we'd get better results if we'd just hope for some good weather.

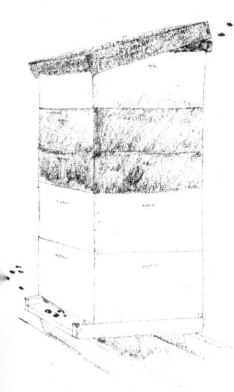

The hot dry spell stayed with us all through July. People's gardens started drying up, the plants got scorched and the vegetables didn't grow. Being by the river, we were luckier than most. Our garden soil is pretty humusy, so it holds the moisture from the river pretty well. It looked dry on top, but when you scuffed it up a little, the dirt underneath was black and moist.

Most of our plants stayed green. They were just a

Sometimes during the hot weather Grandpa will wedge open the top of the hive for added ventilation.

69

little slower growing than they would've been with the rain. We were lucky there, but the bees didn't have it so good. Grandpa was beginning to wonder if we would have a honey crop at all come fall. At the rate they were going, we'd be lucky if they brought in enough honey to last them through the winter.

A couple of afternoons we drove out in the country to check on the beehives Grandpa had farmed out. Each summer he puts some hives in farmers' pastures and orchards for the bees to work the crops. It's a good setup. The bees have a better chance of finding nectar when there aren't too many hives in one place. The farmer likes it because the bees help with the pollination of his fields. And Grandpa gets more honey.

Every time we went out though, we found the same thing. The bees just weren't as busy as Grandpa thought they should be. All the farmers we talked to sounded worried too. Some of them had planted seed three times. The first two plantings rotted, and July was too dry for that third try. "It's been a bad year," they'd say.

We'd talk for a long time with the farmers. Grandpa could feel that they were worried about their crops. He talked to me a lot about farming, thumping along those gravel roads in the old pickup.

"People say the farmer is conservative, Alan. What they really mean when they say that is that they think he's stuck in his ways, slow to change, kind of a dullard, you know?" He said this and looked me right in the eye to make sure I was listening. "They think he's unadventuresome, a stone in the shoe of their newfangled politics.

"Don't let them fool you. As true as I sit here, boy, there's no Las Vegas card shark who puts more on the line than the farmer does. The farmer is the gambler supreme.

"Every spring he gets out there and plows up those fields, planting them full of beans or corn. He doesn't know what price they'll fetch at market. He puts a lot of money into seed and equipment and a variety of chemicals—chemicals of questionable safety if you ask me.

"After he puts out thousands of dollars with no real assurance of his return, he sits and waits and prays that the weather will bring him just the right amount of rain and sunshine for a harvest. The if the market is good, he may just make enough profit to cover his operating costs and see him and his family through the winter. That way next spring he can do it all over again. A man like that has to be crazy or mighty optimistic.

"The Las Vegas card shark has the cards in his hands, but the farmer gambles on things he has absolutely no control over: the weather, insect pests, blight, flood, rodents, anything! It requires all of his financial worth, and he does it year after year. Now that's gambling, wouldn't you say? The farmer is no colorless dullard, Alan. No sirree. Don't let anybody tell you differently!"

Grandpa had a few bee jobs to keep him busy through July. People call him when they find a colony of bees in a building or a barn or someplace like that, and they don't know how to get them out. They really don't know what to do if all of a sudden one day they discover they're sharing their attic or a wall of their house with a colony of bees. Everybody knows that Gramps is the beeman, so they call him up.

Wild bees will build comb and set up housekeeping in any kind of place that will keep their comb dry and protect them from rodents and insects. Hollow trees are great for this, but Grandpa has cleaned bees out of all kinds of places. He's gotten them out of an old bank, from under the floorboards of an abandoned farmhouse, and once from a new house that hadn't even been lived in yet. He's gotten them out of attics, from under eaves and from between the walls of houses.

It's always a sticky job, and he usually doesn't take me along. He gets stung every time because he has to get all the comb out and get the bees set up into a hive body. He says getting stung goes with it. It's a part of the deal.

It has to be warm weather to do a bee job, and it generally takes him three days or more, depending on how tricky a place they're in and how much trouble they give him. It's always a lot of work. Sometimes he has to open up a wall or a floor or a ceiling to get at them. He takes the brood comb out first and sets it in a hive body.

The brood nest is full of babies, so the house bees and the queen will naturally go after it. It's the queen's nursery, and she's got lots of work to do there. Once he gets the brood separated, Grandpa goes back and works at the honeycomb, cleaning it out. Then he puts the comb and bees in boilers and tubs in the back of the pickup. Some bees get crushed, and all of them are fighting mad.

Grandpa gets stung a lot and so does anybody else who happens to be close by. A honeybee can sting a person only once. She dies after that. Whenever somebody here gets stung, there's never very much sympathy to go around. Grandpa or Grandma is always ready to say, "Yeah, but think of the poor bee— she died."

A lot of people have different ideas about bee sting remedies. Grandma says meat tenderizer has worked best for her. Grandpa says that honey works—just a little dab of it right on the spot.

I was stung twice during the summer, once on my eyelid and once on my forehead. I was too close to the hive and got in the way of their fly line. I guess it was mostly my fault. Grandpa says they always go for your eyes because they're shiny.

The sting on my forehead didn't give me much trouble, but the one on my eyelid made my face swell up pretty weirdlike for a couple of days. Both times Grandma put meat tenderizer on them. The second

Grandpa can do a bee job only in warm weather—at least 55 degrees. Here the bees have built their combs in between the rafters of a house. The colony is completely exposed to view, which makes the job of cleaning them out fairly uncomplicated for Gramps.

time we didn't get it on there soon enough I guess. She said that was important—to get it on there right away.

Grandpa brings home all the honey and the comb that he gets from a bee job. In the fall he lets the bees clean out this honey for their winter stores, since honey from a bee job isn't fit for people to eat. Of course, he melts down the wax so he can send it off to Illinois to be recycled into new foundation.

When he finally does get the bees home in the box with their brood nest, it takes three weeks to get them into a proper hive with frames, foundation and supers. He has to wait while the batch of bees in the old brood nest hatch. Then he sets the queen working on new foundation and puts her into a hive body with a queen excluder and supers on top. After that they're just like all his other hives.

One day when Grandpa was out looking into a bee job, I thought I'd found one for him at home. Scott and I were playing with the cats when we saw a huge bumblebee fly into a little round hole in the side of the house. We both ran inside to warn Grandma.

We couldn't find the bee, but we told Grandma about it anyway. She came out to take a look. The hole was there from some old wiring, she said, and the bumblebee had probably built a nest in between the walls.

When Grandpa came home he said it was the queen that we'd seen. "The bumblebee being here is a happy sign for us. She's a hard worker, and we should be glad she's chosen our house to nest in. Her life is a

76

hard one. It's more of a struggle for her than it is for the honeybee.

"That queen lives through the winter all by herself. In the spring she starts laying eggs and building her nest. She forages for pollen and nectar and makes a crude kind of honey to feed to her young brood. Until the young bees are big enough to help her, she maintains the hive all by herself. She doesn't have a very big family, maybe only 20 workers and a few drones.

"But the bumblebee is an important pollinator. She's needed as greatly as the honeybee is, and in some cases she's the only one who can do the pollinating. She has a long tongue that helps her reach down into flowers where a honeybee can't. Red clover is pollinated exclusively by the bumblebee because the nectar is too deep for the honeybee to get."

The cows around here eat a lot of red clover. That made me wonder if the farmers try to get bumblebees to nest around their fields.

"You can't cultivate the bumblebee," Grandpa said. "They're wild things that build nests wherever they can find a hole in the ground or in a building, like this one did here. They make only enough honey for themselves and for the lone queen during the winter, so they haven't been considered of any value to man.

"In fact, bumblebees have been misunderstood by man. For many years the bumblebee was considered a pest like yellow jackets. Both of them can sting you again and again and maybe that's one of the reasons why man has poisoned them and sprayed them and

77

a.   The queen bumblebee is very large—sometimes 2½ to 3 inches-and
difficult to mistake for any other bee. She is very black and very hairy. In
fact she looks quite soft. Worker bumblebees are smaller but are also very
black and downy looking.

b.

b.   The worker honeybee is much smaller than the bumblebee. Her coloring is more brown, but she too has a soft, furry appearance. Pollen dust collects on these minute hairs on the legs and bodies of the bumblebees and honeybees. Thus, they do a great service to man by pollinating his crops.

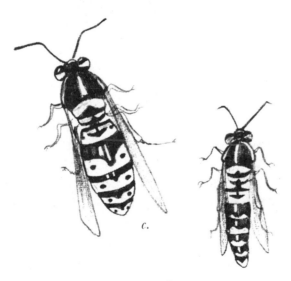

c.

c.   The yellow jacket is a wasp and bears little resemblance to the helpful and hardworking bees. The worker is smaller than the honeybee, and neither the queen (the larger wasp shown here) nor the worker has any fuzz on her body. Their markings are attractive and very black and very yellow.

destroyed their nests trying to exterminate them. That means wipe them out. Now the bumblebee is almost an endangered species. You know what that means. That's the next step to extinction, and extinction is the end of the line. Man treats some of his best friends pretty thoughtlessly, doesn't he, Alan?

"Never kill a bumblebee. Every one of them is precious. If you come across a nest in the ground, put a stake by it for a marker and mow around it. And keep your eyes on that hole over the summer. Make sure our queen stays there. We want her here."

Scott and I watched out for her after that. She came and went a few times each day. After a while smaller bees flew out. We didn't see the queen after that. Grandpa said when the new brood can gather nectar the queen stays in the nest to take care of the new bumblebees.

After everything Grandpa told me about them I almost hoped I'd find another nest. But I never did.

There's one kind of bee job that Grandpa doesn't like to do. That's cleaning out yellow jacket nests. I shouldn't really call it a bee job because yellow jackets aren't bees. They're wasps, and they don't seem to be good for anything. They don't make honey. They don't pollinate plants. They're just ornery pests. They've got a vicious sting, and they attack anybody that comes near their nests. Grandpa always kills the yellow jackets and destroys the nests because if he doesn't, there'll be that many more next year.

"The way they multiply, they'd take over the whole countryside in no time," he says.

Yellow jackets live together in big colonies the way honeybees do. They have one queen who lays all the eggs and a whole army of workers. In the fall the queen lays a lot of queen eggs and drone eggs. When the drones hatch they fertilize the queens. As soon as the cold weather comes, all the drones and the workers die. The new queens are the only ones to winter through, but there might be 50 to 100 of them from one colony. That means 50 to 100 new colonies the next summer. That's what Grandpa means when he says they could take over the whole country.

Each one of these queens from the fall batch finds a protected place under the eaves of a building or under the bark of a tree and hibernates through the winter. In spring they search for places to start new colonies. The queen makes only the beginnings of the nest and lays only a few eggs. These hatch into workers.

After this first brood hatches, the queen stays inside and just lays more eggs. The workers take over her housework, do the food gathering and add on to the nest to make room for the new brood.

Yellow jackets build their nest out of paper. It's a weird-looking thing like a bag hanging down from the eaves of a house or a garage. That's where they like to build if they can, but they build underground too. They find an animal run that's been left empty and make a home in there. Inside the nest the wasps build layers of cells. Sometimes there are only a couple, sometimes four, five, six or seven layers even, stacked up like stories in a building.

It's usually in the fall when yellow jackets are around most. When Grandpa gets a call, he always goes in the daytime first to locate the nest. If it's underground, he follows their fly line to the entrance. If they've built under an eave it's easier to spot them. That big paper nest is hard to miss.

After he finds them he goes back at night when all the wasps are at home and inside the nest. Before he can do anything with them, he has to stun them so they won't attack him. He uses liquid ether, and if they're underground he pours some down the hole. If they're attached to a building, he holds a container of it underneath them, and the fumes go up into the nest. The ether knocks them out only for a little while—just long enough for Grandpa to cut the nest away from the building. As soon as it's down he sets it on fire.

When the nest is underground, he has to dig it completely out to make sure he destroys all of it. By the time he's through, there are usually a few jackets flying around his head. The ether just barely gives him enough time to dig it up. As soon as he sees he's got the whole nest, Grandpa pours gasoline all over the wasps and the cells. That suffocates them and kills all the unhatched larvae.

Grandpa lets me go with him on some of the yellow jacket jobs. I help him with the digging, and if they're in a tricky place, he can use an extra pair of hands. We both wear veils and long pants and long sleeve shirts because neither of us is immune to the yellow jacket sting—it's a lot more powerful than a honeybee's sting. Grandpa told me he's read that some people have really bad reactions to the venom of the yellow jacket, and sometimes they can die from being stung.

I guess he and I aren't that unlucky. We've both been stung and we're still here.

*Exterminating yellow jackets some-
times takes more than one person, so
Grandpa takes Alan along. Here,
the yellow jackets are coming out of
the nest to escape the fumes of the
ether. Alan stands ready with a
knife, so Grandpa can cut the nest
down from the building before they
revive. As soon as it's down,
Grandpa sets the nest on fire to
destroy the wasps and their larvae.*

Grandpa has three brothers. Two of them are farmers. When they come to visit, we get in lots of farm talk about crops, weather and markets. In August, after the rains finally came, Uncle Hilmer was in out of the fields and had time to come see us. He and Gramps inspected the garden and the hives, and I followed them around the yard. Hilmer said our garden was in good shape in comparison to others he'd seen. He agreed that having the river close by probably helped it.

Things like the cauliflower and the cabbage that my mother planted were still small, and it didn't look like we'd get much out of the watermelon patch. But my onions looked good. And we were especially lucky with the squashes. They started growing like weeds after it rained.

Grandma and I stretched out the long arm of one plant and put a stake in the ground at the end of it each night. That way we marked how much it grew in a day. Wow, you should've seen that baby grow—six to ten inches a day after it got a good drink of the rain. Everything in the garden started to take off then.

Every year it seems like one of us has to plant some weird kind of vegetable or flower. The seed catalogue is hard to resist, especially for Grandma. This year she ordered some kind of "Miracle Grow" squash called a guinea bean. It's got huge leaves on it and small white blossoms. It wasn't until it rained that these beans started looking like the pictures in the catalogue: They curled out in great big, long green things and looked like vegetables from outer space. They didn't taste bad though.

Uncle Hilmer thought our sweet corn looked as good as any he'd seen in the county, though that didn't mean it was doing O.K. The rains had come, but it was too late to make juicy kernels of corn. Both Uncle Hilmer and Gramps agreed on that. We didn't get nearly enough out of the plot this year to suit me. I missed those big sweet corn dinners we have every summer.

We walked around the hives, watching the fly lines. Uncle Hilmer taught me a trick with the drones, and I got pretty good at it right away. He showed me how to pick them up by their legs as they come waddling out of the hive. It doesn't hurt them, but they buzz in your hand like mad till you let them go.

I'd seen Grandpa use this trick to joke with some of the people who come to visit. He'd pick up a drone and put it right in his ear and then fold his earlobe over it. The drone would buzz in there, and some people would get pretty excited. They don't always know the difference between a drone and a worker and that a drone doesn't have a stinger. Grandpa's eyes would just pop, and he'd get as big a kick out of it as anybody when he'd let it fly out of his ear. It does look pretty funny. He used to fool me with that trick until I got smart. I was glad Hilmer showed me how to do it. Now I can put a drone in my ear too.

Hilmer said he'd been talking to some other beekeepers who thought their bees were getting ready for a fall honey flow. He thought it might mean that the bees could sense something we couldn't.

"You know how wild creatures are," he said. "They can sometimes sense and understand and get ready for things that we have no awareness of at all."

If it was a fall flow that they were getting ready for, he and Gramps thought it could mean that we'd have a late frost. We'd all like that. I knew the farmers could use the extra growing time for all the seed they planted so late. Of course, the bees would like that extra time to bring in more nectar.

When a worker is loaded with nectar, her abdomen droops as with the bee on the left. When the nectar sac is empty the worker's tail is held high as on the bee at right.

By the middle of August our garden started really looking like a garden. Those guinea beans grew into monster squashes three and four feet long. I'm not exaggerating! Even the melons did all right. We had big juicy muskmelons till I thought. I'd get sick of them. And some of my onions got to be the size of softballs. They get big like that if you put dirt all around them as soon as the tops start to show. It's called hilling up.

The bees finally were busy too. They were working hard in the goldenrod and heartsease that bloom along the roadsides. Grandpa said if they could keep working that way they might be able to make up for the time they lost in July.

When they're busy it's fun to sit next to the entrance of the hive and watch them. They don't even notice you. Field workers bring in so much nectar or pollen that they can hardly fly. They stumble and bump into the hive, while the guard bees inspect them to keep out robbers.

A worker who hatches in the spring and works during the summer doesn't live to see her honey in the fall. When they're working really hard, the worker bees live only about six weeks. New bees that hatch in the fall live the six months through the winter because they eat less and don't grow to complete adults.

"It's a sort of suspended animation," Gramps says. "Just one of the many ingenious methods Nature has

devised to take care of those who need special atten-
tion to get through the winter months."

I've tried to count the bees as they come into the
hive, but it's impossible. With the fanners in front of
the hive, the new bees coming and going, and the
house bees doing their chores, it's too confusing to
keep track. Still, Grandpa says it's highly organized.

"Those fanners in front are fanning fresh air into
the hive to help keep it the right temperature inside
and evaporate the moisture out of the nectar. Inside
fanners are working too, but they're fanning stale air
out of the hive. It's amazing that they can control that,
isn't it? They're a smart bunch of girls. They know
how to keep the humidity just right."

Humidity is the amount of moisture in the air.
When people say it's a muggy day, they're talking

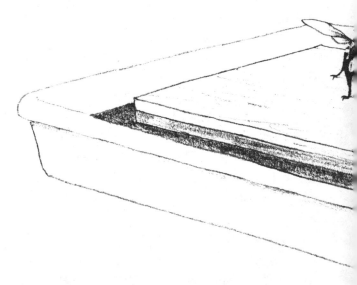

*Even with the river nearby, Grandpa will put out watering pans during
dry weather. He always floats a piece of board in the water so the bees
have something to ride on while they drink.*

about the humidity. Or if they say they can't breathe because the air is so heavy, it's the humidity that's getting to them. It's what makes some people's hair go curly and some people's go straight.

"When it's dry like it was in July, some of those field workers have to go out and bring in water in their nectar sacs. It's not easy finding puddles in a dry season, but the bees' antennae are sensitive to any source of water around them, and they can fly right to it," Gramps said.

Our bees are lucky. They have the river right out here, but they have to be careful that they don't fall in and make a nice sweet snack for a frog or a lizard or some bird that happens to be there at the same time.

"When they bring the water back," Grandpa went on, "they give it to one of the house bees. She takes it

and puts a little dot of it here and there on the honeycomb. Then as the fanners work, air circulates through the hive and the water evaporates, cooling the air. It makes for an ingenious and highly effective air conditioning system.

"The bees have been doing it for centuries. So if anybody ever asks you who really invented the air conditioner, I guess you've got an original answer, right?"

Gramps has a keen way of looking at the bees. It's like one of the books I checked out of the library this summer with one page full of Interesting Facts About The Bees. It was pretty amazing. Listen to this: Bees can fly at speeds up to 15 miles per hour and go as far away from home as 10 to 15 miles to get nectar.

When a field worker goes out, she's usually gone for about an hour and she'll visit maybe 50 flowers in that time. It takes about 30,000 of these trips to make one pound of honey. As Grandma says, that's 30,000 bees working for one hour to make one pound. That's a fact to boggle your brain, isn't it?

In late summer our regular customers begin coming around to see about the honey crop. They put in their orders or bring their jars for us to refill, and Grandma starts washing a few dozen of our own to get ready for when we extract.

Washing jars is Grandma's job. It's not such a bad job if we all chip in, so she always tries to get us to help. I don't like to come inside, but Grandma is smart. She saves it for a rainy day.

The new jars we ordered in the spring and any old jars that we'll use for ourselves have to be washed in hot soapy water. I'm good at drying because my hand is small and can fit inside the jar to dry the corners. Drying the jars is important because if any moisture touches the honey at all, the honey will sour. The jars look nice and polished too when they're dried well.

The bees keep moisture out of their honey with the cappings. Gramps says honeycomb is the ideal way to store honey. It can last for years in the comb. The cells are small and separated, so if somehow moisture gets into one cell or a capping gets opened, the whole comb isn't soured.

That's the same reason Grandpa doesn't like to package his honey in containers any bigger than five pounds. Some people like to have their honey in gallon jugs, but Grandpa tells them he won't fill gallons. He figures if a jar breaks or spills, it's better not to lose so much at one time.

I'll have to agree with him there. Once I accidentally dropped a five pounder on the way from the honey house. I felt sick about it, but the bees came and cleaned it up for me. That's the advantage to living in an apiary I guess. At least honey isn't wasted.

When Grandma starts washing jars, it's a sure sign that Grandpa is going to be extracting soon. Usually he's out in the honey house working away into November, but this fall was different. He decided to get an early start, and everything was done by the middle of October.

...oney house is used for storage
...g the winter. The extractor is
...ed with towelling to keep the
...out of it. A pan of cappings
...ns to be melted down for recy-
... Extracted supers will be
...ed in the spring and added to
...ves as they are needed.

Grandpa is proud of his honey house. He's had it for years. When he moved into town 20 years ago, he brought it with him. And when he moved to this place by the river, he picked it up and brought it along again.

Inside are the extractor and work tables, an old heating stove, shelves of bee supplies and usually a few supers. He keeps all his new foundation on the shelves and the old wax in bricks on the tables. Cases of honey jars are stacked up against one wall almost to the ceiling, and our work aprons and a fly swatter hang on the hooks next to the door. It's a clean honey house.

He has a scale to weigh the jars that people bring him, even though he can almost always tell what a jar will hold. But guessing doesn't make for good business, he says. Sometimes he weighs a frame both before and after he's extracted it to find out how much honey was in the comb.

Grandpa had a spell of laudatory oratory once and told me, "The thing I like best about this old honey house is the way it smells. That rich, sweet, fullsome aroma of comb and honey overtakes me, makes me feel heady and light and some kind of special. It's a completely invigorating and captivating aroma—like the way the smell of bread baking turns your head around, makes you stop and breathe in deep servings of it.

"The sweetness of every summer for the past 30 years is preserved in this honey house. You can smell it, can't you, boy?"

I sure can. Sometimes I think my clothes will absorb some of that aroma and my blue jeans and my shirt will smell like Grandpa's, but it never works. It must take years to smell like that. I think when my clothes do smell like honey, I'll know I'm a real beekeeper.

The extracting work starts out in the hives. We always work on a nice sunny day while the bees are away from home. We both put on our bee veils, and I hold the smoker while Grandpa opens the hive.

He wedges his hive tool between the frames and carefully gets a hold on them. One by one he pulls them out and gives each one a quick jerk in front of the hive. The bees fall off on to the ground and Grandpa puts the frame without any bees on it into an empty super. The shakeup doesn't bother the bees. They just pick themselves up and go back into the hive while we get away with the honey.

Grandpa takes several supers into the honey house at a time, but he keeps the different kinds of honey separate. He likes clover honey to taste like clover honey with no dandelion mixed in, and he likes fruit blossom honey to be fruit blossom and that's all.

He can tell what kind of honey is in each super by the color and taste of it. And if you ask him just when he put each super on each hive, he can tell you right off. I don't know how he can keep all that in his brain. He remembers everything.

Alan holds the smoker while Grandpa opens the hive.

The bees hate to see their honey go, and sometimes a few will follow us up to the honey house. But this August when we started collecting supers, we didn't have to work too hard to keep the bees out. Grandpa said it was a sure sign there was a honey flow on. If they're too busy to follow us with the honey, it means they're out there finding nectar in the fields.

Once we get into the honey house with the supers and we put our aprons on, the real work begins. Grandpa does most of it because it takes a lot of skill to do a good job. He uses a capping knife with a very sharp two-edged blade to cut into the wax. He heats it in a pan of water over a hot plate, so it can melt the wax a little when he slices through it.

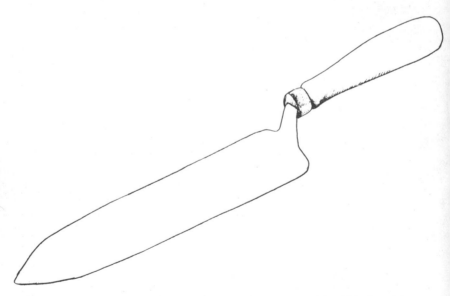

The capping knife has a very sharp, double-edged blade.

Cutting the cappings off can be tricky. He holds the frame just so with his left hand over a large pan. Then with the knife he shaves off the cappings that seal the honeycomb. When the blade is sharp and hot, the cappings come off like the lid off a can and fall into the pan in sheets with honey dripping all over them.

Grandpa makes it look really easy. He says there's an air space right underneath the cappings. The trick is to get the blade under there and let it glide along. Well, I know it's not that easy because I tried it just once. I couldn't find the air pocket, and I gouged out the comb so badly that Grandpa didn't let me finish.

It's important not to cut into the honeycomb, so the frames can go right back into the supers and back to the bees in good shape. If the comb is gouged or cut unevenly, the bees have to repair it. And since it takes honey to make the wax, that means extra work and wasted time for them.

After a frame is uncapped Grandpa puts it in the extractor. That's where I come in. The extractor is a big metal tank that's open at the top and has a spigot at the bottom. Inside the tank are two long, thin wire baskets that the frames just fit into. They hang opposite each other on a shaft. A motor turns the shaft and spins the baskets around. My job is running this motor.

It's the spinning that draws the honey out of the comb. Grandpa says the extractor works the same way that a merry-go-round does when you get it going

The extractor is cleaned once every year. Before he starts extracting in the fall, Grandpa thoroughly rinses the extractor with cold water. The belt around the wheel at the right connects to a motor.

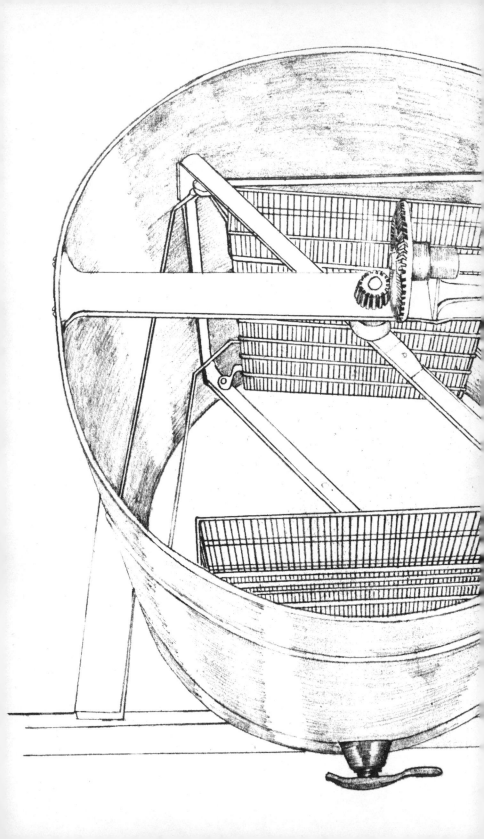

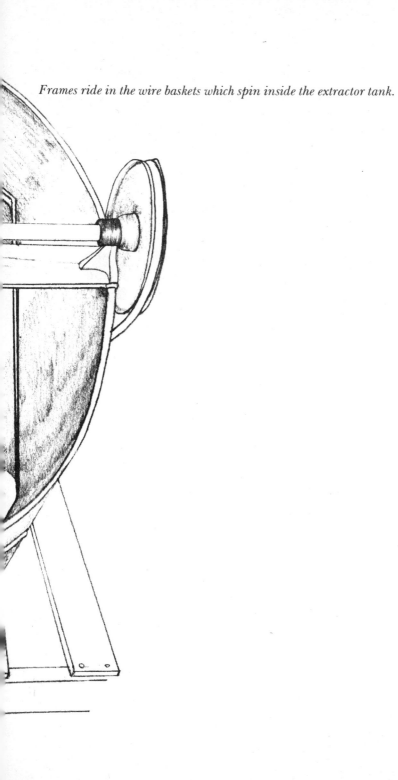

Frames ride in the wire baskets which spin inside the extractor tank.

really fast and you get the feeling something is pulling you to the edge. In the same way, the honey is thrown against the inside of the tank, drips down the sides and collects in the bottom.

You have to know just how long to leave the frames spinning. It doesn't take even a minute. If they spin too long, the force will crush the comb. If they don't spin long enough, we don't get all the honey out. It has to be just right.

When Grandpa signals me to stop—sometimes I have to remind him to signal—I turn the motor off and wait for the baskets to stop spinning. Then I lift the frames out and turn them over because the spinning only takes the honey out of one side at a time. When that's done I turn the motor on and wait for Grandpa's signal again.

When the comb is clean, he takes the extracted frames and puts them right back in the same order in the same super that they came from, and we start again. That's our system, and we can extract about 100 pounds in three hours working like this. That's not bad, huh?

With the door closed to keep the bees out and the hot plate turned on, the honey house gets really warm. That's why I like to extract later in the fall. When the honey house is warm on those frosty nights, it's the right time for drinking in that fresh honey aroma, as Grandpa says. It doesn't even seem like work really.

The extractor tank fills up to a certain level under

the baskets, and Grandpa drains the honey out into a big steel pot with a spigot on it. He puts the pot on a stand over another hot plate and heats the honey just a little bit so that any wax that got into it will float to the top. We don't want any wax in our honey. People don't like that.

There's a thermometer attached to this pot to make sure that the honey doesn't get too hot. Grandpa has told me a hundred times, "Heat is a terrible thing for honey. Too much of it destroys all that's good about this precious liquid—all the enzymes and things that make it good for you, not to mention the flavor.

"Honey that's been overheated tastes bad. Most of that stuff on the grocer's shelf has been burned. Big commercial honey producers do that to keep it from granulating—though there's nothing wrong with granulated honey; it has a flavor all its own. If you ever taste some of that commercial honey, you'll know what I mean. You can't believe it could be the same golden nectar we've got here. They just ruin it."

Grandpa likes to brag about his honey. People have brought him honey from all over the United States and some foreign countries too, but he says he's never tasted any honey as good or as pure as his own. I'll take his word for it, and I know other people who'll back him up.

When the honey has been warmed just a little bit— just about body temperature—the wax floats to the top, and the honey is ready to go into the jars. We've got a special way to do that too. I hand Grandpa a

Honey that has no comb in it is called extracted honey.

Cut comb honey is honey that is still in the comb. The honeycomb is cut out of the frames and put into jars. Extracted honey is poured over the cut comb to fill the jar and keep the wax from drying out.

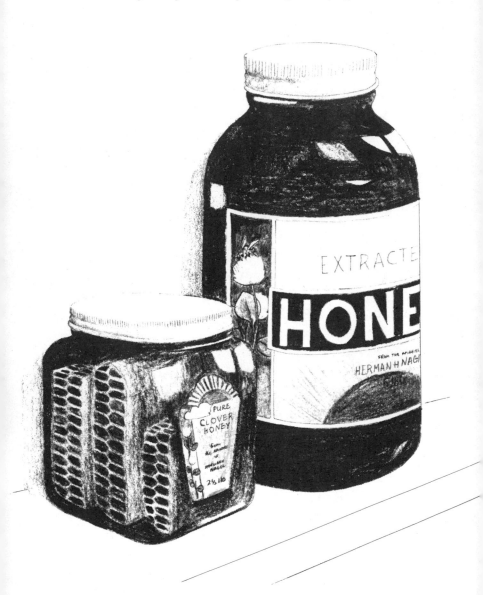

clean jar, and he fills it from the spigot, holding the jar tilted so the honey streams down the side of the jar. That way there aren't any bubbles in the honey. It's just absolutely clear and golden.

After the first jar is full, Grandpa always holds it up to the light. Every year he takes it and admires it like it's the first honey he ever saw.

"It's true inspiration," he says. "Just marvel at it. Look at it and marvel. Think about where it came from, how it got here. The distilled nectar from an unthinkable, uncountable number of blooms and blossoms, made for you here for your palatable pleasure through the unselfish and wholehearted industries of a combined sisterhood of hundreds of thousands of willing laborers.

"We've bottled summer. Here is the very essence of its fields and pastures, green meadows and golden acres. Think on it and marvel!"

He's right too, you know. When we get it in the jars and those golden bottles are lined up all over the work tables and shelves, the honey house is full with the smell of it. And that's what I see: bottled summer.

Grandpa didn't have too many cut comb supers this year. They're usually shallow supers, and the foundation in them is completely wax. For cut comb the foundation has to be all wax without plastic or wire, since each frame is taken out and the comb completely cut away from the frame. That way you get a long brick of honey to slice into sections for bottling.

Some folks ask for cut comb especially because they like it or because it's good for their allergies or hay fever. Grandpa has customers who get a couple of pounds of cappings for the same reasons.

I like both comb honey and the cappings. They're good and chewy. They're especially good spread on toast. It's easy to eat the wax that way. By itself it's kind of hard to swallow.

Grandpa says the wax is good for you, so Grandma mixes up the cappings and comb honey into a kind of candy with ground up sunflower seeds, nuts, and raisins. It's really delicious. I could eat it all the time, but she makes it only on special days.

The early start Grandpa got with the extracting was nice for a change. There wasn't a whole lot of honey, but he figured he'd have enough to fill orders for regular customers. He wasn't counting on enough to take to the grocery store, and he said he wouldn't put up the COMB AND EXTRACTED HONEY FOR SALE sign.

"There's no use attracting business we can't take

care of," he said. "We can thank our lucky stars and the bee goddess in heaven for that late summer honey flow, Alan. It's the only reason the bees have any honey to spare at all. Better pray for a late frost, so they can keep building up those winter stores for themselves."

It seems like he must have jinxed things when he said that because the next week, in late September, we got that killer frost. The beans were all limp on the vines and the melons turned squashy overnight. No more muskmelons after school. And I thought about all the fall vegetable stews I'd miss without that garden produce. No more eggplant parmigiana and zucchini fritters.

I felt bad for the bees too. No more nectar for them in the fields. The first hard frost always marks the end of the season.

"It's a temperamental business when you're a partner with the weather," Grandpa said. "Thank goodness again for that September honey flow. Hilmer wasn't right about the late frost, but I guess maybe he was onto something when he said the bees could sense something brewing.

"Bless those creatures. They worked when they could, and if winter means to come and stay right now, those girls have a long haul in front of them." That's how Grandpa summed up the whole disaster.

That morning the news was full of talk about the frost and what it would mean to the farmers. It was pretty bad. Some late plantings weren't ripe yet, and

111

some farmers lost whole fields. That meant they lost lots of money too.

Grandpa's honey crop this year was right around 2,000 pounds. He filled all the orders from our regular customers and put away our own winter store of about 120 pounds. I always think we should put away more, but I guess I don't know what amount would sound like enough to me. We stored our own in three-pound jars. Grandma says that's a good size for using in the kitchen or on the table.

The last couple of years we've had enough honey to put in the back of the truck and take to farm sales on Saturdays. We'd take a couple of cases of cut comb and extracted honey, and we'd set them on the tailgate of the pickup.

Almost every weekend during the nice weather there are ads in the newspaper saying "Farm Sale." The way Grandpa explains it to me is that a lot of small farmers who own 120 acres or so are retiring, or they can't afford to compete with the big farmer anymore.

"Their sons have grown up, gone to school, moved to the city, and don't want farm life, so these farmers have to sell," he says.

Sometimes they've already sold the land to that big farmer, and what's left for sale is just some machinery, tools and household things. Sometimes they sell everything: house, barn, tools, machines, land and all.

"At some of these sales a man may see his whole life, everything he's been working for over the years, sold to a pack of strangers in an afternoon. A farm sale has got a lot of mixed feelings in it for that reason." Grandpa sure makes it sound like serious business, doesn't he? I think they're fun.

All kinds of people go to the sales. Most are farmers in overalls looking for a good deal on farm machinery. Some are men in business suits. Grandpa says they're land developers and speculators. "Got a lot of money in their pockets to buy up all this glorious countryside, dig in artificial lakes and put up those fandangled condominiums all around them. They ought to be chased out of the county on sight for the common criminals they are. They rob the country of its natural, quiet, and dignified pastorale."

There are always just-married people looking for good used furniture, and usually there are some fancy-looking people all dressed up, women in high heels and men in ties. They've got lots of money, Grandpa says. "They're antique dealers and they can make it pretty rough on the newlyweds and anybody else looking for a bargain. They can afford to outbid just about anybody on the furniture because they buy the farmer's four-poster bed, take it back to the city and sell it for double or triple what they paid for it. Don't let them fool you; they know what they're doing."

Whole families go to the sales too, just for the fun of it like we do. In some of these small towns the farm sale may be the biggest doings of the weekend. There's usually some kind of snack served or maybe even whole meals, so it's easy to spend the day.

I like selling the honey from the back of the truck. People are always coming around asking us about our business. Sometimes we run into a fellow who keeps bees too, and then he and Gramps get to talking. There's nothing to stop beemen once they start swapping bee stories.

A few times those antique dealers have bought honey from us. I always wondered if they took it back to the city and sold it for more money.

Every year in the fall when we're through extracting I like to go to the farm sales, but this year Grandpa said we wouldn't have enough extra to sell that way. We got rid of it all through orders. I missed

114

those Saturdays, but if I thought more from the bees' point of view I'd just hope for enough honey to last through the winter.

October started out pretty cold and dreary but turned into a great fall month. It got sunny and warm and stayed that way. The bees were out flying every day looking for nectar. They didn't find much, but they did bring in some pollen. Whenever it's warm and sunny they like to be out.

"They're just like you, Alan," Grandpa says. "They want to be outside too. They like to work."

Since there wasn't any nectar for them, we had to keep an eye out for robber bees. A few bees from a hive may go out scouting around their neighbors looking for a weak hive or one with some lazy guards.

115

It can be a pretty funny show watching those bees trying to get into another hive.

Grandpa told me, "Once a robber bee always a robber bee. Once a worker takes to a life of crime she'll never go out into the fields again. She's had a taste of that 'get rich quick life' and savored the immoral joys of a ready-made product, so why go to all that work of nectar gathering?

"You can always tell a robber bee. She's a tawdry old thing, doesn't have any fuzz left on her anymore. Her wings are a might battered too because she's been in a lot of scrapes at a lot of doorways."

It takes a little patience to sit at the hive and watch for robber bees, but this fall it didn't take long. That early frost and the warm weather made it perfect for robbing. I'd sit there in the afternoon, and pretty soon one of these shifty girls would land off to one side of the entryway. She'd be there for a minute or a half an hour depending on whether she tried to bolt through the guards or to be sly and fake it as one of the hive's sisters. When she gets up to the entrance it's up to the guards to check her out and send her away. Most often that's what happens.

Sometimes a robber can be extra crafty or extra lucky, and she can slip by the guards when they're booting out another robber. Grandpa says he's seen robber bees actually take posts as fanners at the entrance of the hive, so they can look like real workers and gradually work their way closer and closer and finally get into the hive. Sometimes robbers can find a hole or a crack in a super and get in that way too.

116

If they ever do get in and none of the workers inside catches them, when they get out again it's a disaster for the hive. The robber takes her loot with her back to her own hive and tells all her sisters about this great source of ready-made honey she's found. After the frost in the fall, that's just what the bees like to hear. And pretty soon the hive that was raided is black with other robbers.

In a place like Grandpa's where there are so many bees together, this kind of thing can turn into a real nightmare. Thousands of bees can die defending their stores, and there's almost no way to help them either. You just have to wait till night when the robbers all go home and hope it doesn't start up the next day. Grandpa says that sometimes whole hives are completely wiped out this way.

I've never seen this happen and I hope I never do, but it's fun to watch a robber try to get through. Our hives are in good shape, our bees are strong, and the guards do a pretty good job, I guess. Grandpa helps by repairing the cracks and holes in warped or damaged supers. It sure pays in the long run.

In the fall the workers force the drones out of the hive.

When the nectar flows are over, the queen slows down her egg laying and the workers begin to get ready for winter. The first thing they do is trim down the size of their family. All the old bees and the drones have to go. The winter stores are too valuable to use up on bees that are old and can't do any work anymore, and the hive will hatch all new drones in the spring anyway.

The old workers who couldn't live through the winter leave the hive and go away to die or just never make it home from their last field trip. The bees can't stand to have dead bees in the hive, so, as Grandpa says, these old girls still do their part for the colony by finding a place to die away from the hive. This way they save their sisters the trouble of having to haul them out.

The drones are another story. The workers won't let them get to any of the honey stores, so it's a slow starvation for them. It sounds terrible, but if the workers didn't get rid of the drones the hive might not have enough honey to last through the winter. The drones would eat too much.

When they're weak from not eating, the drones are lugged outside the hive and dropped over the edge. I can't see how the workers do it, since the drones are so much bigger than they are. But I've seen them by the dozens flying out of the hive carrying the drones away.

119

For a while the ground in front of the hive is just loaded with dead and dying drones, until they're eaten or carried away by other animals or insects. Raccoons like the taste of bees, and they come up from the river at night for a real feast at this time of year.

I came home from school one afternoon, and Grandpa was looking in on one of the hives. When I say looking in, I mean just that. He'd given some old comb from a bee job to one of the lighter weight hives and then put a piece of window glass under the hive cover. Whenever he took off the cover, we could see what the bees were doing just as if we were inside the hive. They were all over that old comb, cleaning it out and putting the honey into their winter stores.

"Now is the time to feed them: on these beautiful fall days, when they'd like to be out working anyway. Let them store it up for the winter. There've been a few envious bees with robber potential flying around here. Now watch this." As he said this, Grandpa slid the glass back just enough to make an entrance. When he did it, some guard bees were right there at the opening and none of the robbers got in.

I could watch the glass hive all day. The bees go right on working the same as if they were all covered up. You can see them cleaning out that old comb and crawling all over each other.

"All that jostling and nudging is part of the hive communication," Gramps said. "They're feeding each other and passing along the news of the day. That's how they all know each other so well and can recognize the strange odor of any robber bees hovering outside."

Grandpa fed them all a lot during the warm part of October. It's best to feed them then. They can put the honey in their comb. That's the natural place for them to feed during the winter.

Some of the honey that Grandpa feeds them he gets from melting down the cappings after we extract. Of course, he sends the wax away to make new foundation. At $1.35 a pound, beeswax is valuable stuff. It sure looks valuable too all stacked up on shelves in the honey house.

Grandpa made a special contraption for melting down the cappings. It looks like a little slide with high sides on it. He puts a hot plate underneath the higher end and a deep pan at the lower end. Then he scoops the cappings up and puts them over the heat at the

121

top of the slide. As the honey gets warm, it runs down the slide into the pan. The wax melts more slowly and drips down on top of the honey.

In the pan the wax floats, and as it cools it hardens. When the pan is full, it's like the honey has a lid of wax on it. It's like the paraffin seal on Grandma's jellies.

One day in October Grandpa set honey out in pans for the bees to gather up. We mixed it with a little water and draped clean cloths over it. The cloth sits on top of the honey, so the bees have something to ride on while they drink up the honey.

It took them a while to get started. It was morning and still cool. At first just the bees from the closest hives found it. A couple of them fell into the puddle in the middle of the cloth, where the honey was thick and sticky because of the cold. They got coated in honey and couldn't crawl out, so I picked them up and put them down at their hive.

Right away a couple of house bees hurried out and started licking them off, cleaning them and helping them dry their wings. They were fine, but they both sat at the doorstep in the sunlight for a few minutes before they went inside. They must have done the bee dance and spread the word because it wasn't long before that pan had bees all over it.

By noon all the pans were full of bees, and they were backed up in the air over the pans "like planes waiting to land at O'Hare Field." That's what Grandpa said they looked like.

On the comb the bees work very close to one another, jostling and crawling over each other. The hive communicates this way. The two bees at the
left are communicating with their antennae and are about to pass food
from one to the other.

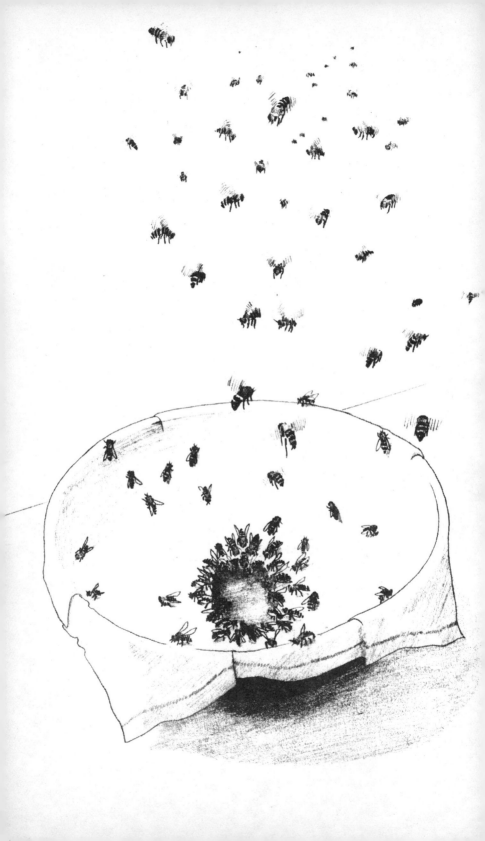

It was nice to see them so busy and glad to be working. Grandpa thought they looked so preoccupied with their business that we could pick them up and carry them to town without them knowing it.

He was exaggerating, but we did try a little experiment. It showed me just how accurate their flying instructions are. We moved one of the pans to see how long it would take the bees to find it in a new spot. We put it about six feet away from where it had been.

Sure enough, pretty soon there was a batch of bees circling and buzzing around the old place looking for that honey. It took them half an hour to find the pan in the new spot.

At four o'clock in the afternoon there were a few bees still looking for honey even though they'd licked those pans shiny clean. There were a couple of dead bees in the cloths, but Grandpa said that they were probably old bees anyway who'd gotten too heavy with honey and couldn't lift themselves up.

After that day most of the hives were richer in winter stores by as much as a pound, depending on the size of the colony and how many workers they had to bring the honey in. It felt good to see them have an easy day like that. With all that honey it must have been a real picnic for them.

After the frost in the fall or in the early spring, if the hives feel light, Grandpa will feed them. He mixes honey and a little water and puts it in a large bowl with a cloth draped over it. The cloth floats on top of the honey and helps to keep the bees from drowning while they drink from the pool in the middle of the cloth. Many bees are backed up in the air over the bowl waiting for their turn to feed.

By November all the extracting was done. Grandpa had picked up the supers that had been out in the country all summer, and he did all the extracting for Mr. Fields and Elton Howding. They're two beekeepers around here who don't have their own extractors, so they bring all their supers to Gramps.

Almost everyone had come and picked up their orders, too, except for the Millers, Mr. Link, and Old Man Mossert down the road from us. He's always the last to get his even though he lives close by.

I know all this because I help Grandma a little with the bookwork. It's her job to see that the books are balanced. That means keeping track of who owes what and sending out the bills. I put the stamps on the envelopes and address some of them. I think I like Grandpa's end of the work better because I'm not much good at figures.

This year we charged 60 cents a pound for honey in the new jars and 45 cents a pound if people brought their own jars to be filled. That's a good price, Grandma said, but she can remember when they first started selling honey 35 years ago, it was 25 cents a pound.

Grandpa says that yields were better then, and that made the price lower. He says it wasn't unusual for each hive to average between 125 to 175 pounds in a season. Not bad, huh? This year he averaged 70 pounds a hive. My own hive did all right with 90 pounds. We feel lucky though because the state average was only 50 pounds per hive.

What with all that rain in June, the drought in July and the early frost, we can be thankful for anything we got. I guess the farmers feel the same way. Most of them around here didn't come out as badly as they did in some other parts of the state, but yields were down everywhere. It just wasn't a year for growers.

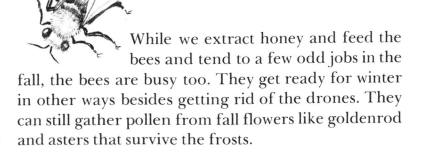

While we extract honey and feed the bees and tend to a few odd jobs in the fall, the bees are busy too. They get ready for winter in other ways besides getting rid of the drones. They can still gather pollen from fall flowers like goldenrod and asters that survive the frosts.

127

They use a lot of propolis at this time and fly out to gather all kinds of gummy stuff like oil paint, varnish, coal tar, or sap from trees. Propolis is made out of this sticky stuff, and the bees winterproof their hives with it. They glue shut all the cracks and holes. Sometimes they coat the whole inside of the hive to make extra sure there aren't any places for the wind or snow to get in.

They might start to close up the entryway with it too (like drawing a curtain) to keep out mice and the weather. It's good glue. Grandpa says the only thing that will take it off your hands is rubbing alcohol. Soap and water don't touch it. That's why we have to scrub so hard in the spring to get it off those old supers.

On the frames house workers move the honey stores in close to the brood nest so it's easy to get at during the winter. Waxmakers seal up all the pollen and honey cells airtight, so no moisture can get it and spoil it.

Bees don't hibernate in the wintertime like some animals, but when the temperature drops below 57 degrees—from about November to April around here—they start forming their winter cluster. Grandpa says clustering is a pretty clever method of keeping warm.

He told me, "Bees are cold-blooded creatures by themselves, but in the winter cluster they act together like one warm-blooded animal. They all group together toward the center of the hive body, some of

Bees never sleep. Even in winter they are semiactive. They form a ball in the middle of the comb and huddle close together. By slight vibrating movements they generate enough heat to keep themselves warm. This winter action is called clustering.

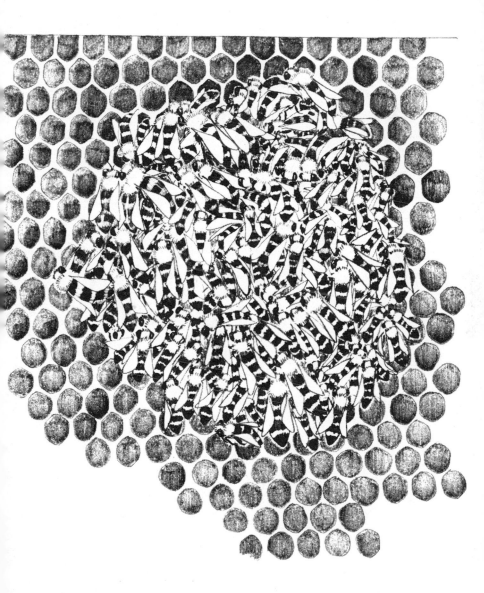

After Alan and Grandpa have raked the leaves in the fall, they pack them around the bottoms of the hives to form insulation against the winter winds.

them backed into empty brood cells, others on top of them. The colder the temperature the more closely they cluster. Then by slight vibrating movements and by feeding each other, they generate enough heat to keep themselves comfortable. Those bees closest to the stores start a feeding chain that eventually reaches those on the very outside of the huddle.

"Clustering is a wonder they've developed over the eons. Even though it may be below zero outside the hive and just a few inches from the ball of bees, if they have enough food they'll be able to keep the temperature between 68 and 96 degrees.

"It sounds simple, doesn't it? If they eat just enough, move just right and stick together, they'll be warm. But it's more complex, more ingenious and sophisticated than just that. Not only do they keep themselves warm with this cluster, but they regulate the air flow out of the hive that takes with it all the waste gases and excess water vapor.

"Bees never sleep, Alan. They work the year round," Grandpa said. "Yes sir, she's a real girl wonder, the honeybee. A true miracle of evolutionary ingenuity, don't you think?"

I was glad when he told me about the winter cluster. It was hard to believe how those little insects could stay outside all winter and last through it. It gets below zero a lot here, and we always have a couple of bad storms. In some places like Canada they take the hives inside for the winter or pack them to keep them warm.

It's better not to do that if you don't have to, Gramps says, because on warm winter days the bees need to get out for their cleansing flights. If they're all wrapped up and they want to get out, they may get restless and that's never good.

We don't pack our hives, but we rake leaves underneath and around the bottoms of them. Grandpa built a board fence behind some of the hives to act as a windbreak. We make sure all the hives have both inner and outer covers on them, and, of course, Grandpa lifts them all a little to see that they're "heavy enough" with food for the winter. Other than that, there's not much we can do.

I always hope and pray for them a lot and think about them.

After everybody has picked up their orders, all the rest of the honey is for our use during the coming year. Grandpa keeps it right out in the honey house until we need it. Honey should be stored in a cool dark place, but not in a damp basement. If light shines on the bottles, the honey will darken and lose some of its fresh taste. Heat and moisture will spoil it too. The honey house is a perfect storage place, but it sure seems like a long way from the house.

I wish we could find room for it inside. I'd like to look at it more, and I keep thinking if we run out of honey in the house during a blizzard, it would be kind of hard to get out to the honey house. But when I ask Grandma about it she just teases me and says I eat too much of it anyway. I eat it on everything I can think of: toast, ice cream, chocolate milk, crackers, popcorn, sunflower seeds, peanut butter, fruit salads, cheese. Maybe that's why they keep it all the way out there.

When November comes and we've done all we can for the bees, there's not much to do but sit and wait for the first snow. Grandma always says the first snow comes with Thanksgiving and the last one with Easter. She surely was right about Thanksgiving this year. We had a blizzard. Uncle Hilmer and Aunt Letty were here for turkey and pumpkin pie made from pumpkin from our garden. They almost got snowbound with us.

134

There were lots of snowmobiles making all kinds of racket on the road and in the woods around us till all hours of the night during the blizzard. "They disturb the serenity of the winter landscape and the peaceful sleep of all wildlife," Grandpa said.

The sky cleared after a day and a half, and Scott and I took our sleds to the park. When we got home Grandpa was out checking around the hives. He says the snow helps to insulate the hives if it doesn't block the entryways, so he was sweeping it away from there. I went to see if I could help and if the bees survived the first cold.

Gramps was bent over one of the hives, and he motioned to me, "Come here, Alan. Take a whiff of this."

I put my face down close to the entryway of my hive. Warm air and a strong smell of warm honey was coming out. I could even see a few bees walking around in there. Grandpa said that was because the sun had been warming the hive. I was convinced then that the winter cluster really does work to warm the bees. That blast of warm air made me sure of it.

When I put my ear next to the hive, I could hear a faint hum, like the one you hear when you put a seashell to your ear, and the sound of the ocean is inside. It was the movement of the bees in their cluster.

We checked all the hives, and every one of them seemed O.K. At one I knocked around a little too much and the buzzing got louder like a dull roar.

"They're alive all right. Don't rile them too much,

Alan put his ear to the hive and could hear the hum of the winter cluster.

Alan," Grandpa said. "If they feel the need to come out and investigate, they may catch cold." We left them alone then, and they quieted down right away.

When we went inside Grandma fixed some hot spearmint tea for us. Every year she dries the mint from the yard. It makes delicious tea, especially with a little honey in it. While we were sitting there, she asked me what it was time to start thinking about now that Thanksgiving was behind us. I knew what she meant. Every year we send honey to all our relatives and friends for Christmas. Grandma likes to get things done early because we have to send most of it by the mail.

"The list will be shorter this year," she said, "since our harvest wasn't as big as usual."

It seemed long enough to me as I wrote down everybody she named: Uncle Hilmer and Aunt Letty, Uncle Jack and Aunt Corrine, Cousin Bella and Billy.

"Don't forget Grandma Edelston. She needs it for her rheumatism," Grandma said, and then added about ten more people.

We put the honey in tins that Grandpa soldered shut, wrapped red ribbon around them and then boxed them up for mailing. I like sending the honey out. I think it makes a really nice present. At least I wouldn't mind getting it in the mail.

The snow stayed on the ground after Thanksgiving. All of December we were busy with Christmas things, and there wasn't much beekeeping to do. January and February are slow months for a beekeeper too. About the only thing to do is look through the bee catalogues. This winter I don't need to do that. For Christmas Grandma and Grandpa gave me a brand-new bee veil and a hive tool of my own.

I gave them a subscription to a bee magazine. When the first issue came in the mail, it took us a few days to look it over. There were a lot of pictures of bees up really close in their hives and pollinating flowers and things like that. One article in the magazine was about how amazing it was that bees could fly at all. It said that their bodies are really to big for such fragile, little wings like they have. I'd never thought about that before.

The magazine had interesting stories about bees and beekeeping from all over the world. There were pictures of a little tiny bee that lives in Africa and South America and is stingless. Now that sounds like some kind of bee, doesn't it?

I read another thing that I thought was pretty nifty. It said that for one pound of honey the bees put in 50,000 miles of flying. In other words, they fly the distance around the world twice, gathering nectar that makes one pound of honey.

I started thinking about all the honey we extracted this fall, all the honey that's out there in the hives right now, plus all the honey the bees ate during the summer. It's plain to see how much work went into it. I guess I know now why Grandpa thinks so much of his bees and why he likes to talk about what "unique and strangely marvelous creatures" they are. He's really right. I'll be glad when the spring comes, and we can get back outside and work with them again.

I suppose I'll always want to keep bees. Grandpa says it's something that gets into your system. "I can't imagine not having bees. There's so much to learn from them," he says.

He's had bees ever since he was my age, so I guess I've got a lot of things to find out yet. "You've got a good start on you," he told me. "But just take the years as they come. Right now we've got to think about making it through the next six weeks.

"March is a fierce month and a crucial one for the bees. If they can make it through March and their stores hold out through the first of April, we should be O.K. That's how you've got take it with beekeeping—just day to day, patiently." If anybody would know my Grandpa would.

I'm just finding out, and I've still got a long way to go. But when my blue jeans smell like honeycomb and my jacket pocket always has a hive tool in it, I guess then I'll know for sure that I really and truly am a beekeeper.